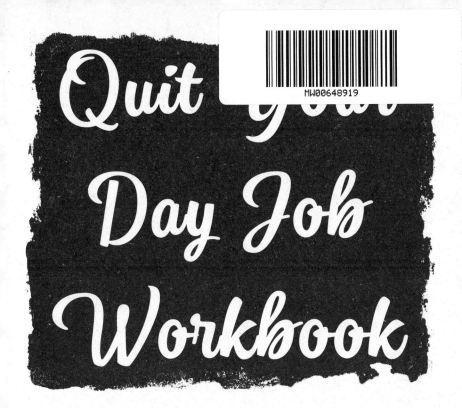

Quit Your Day Job Workbook

Eleanor C. Whitney, MPA

Quit Your Day Job Workbook

BUILDING THE DIY PROJECT, LIFE, AND BUSINESS OF YOUR DREAMS

Eleanor C. Whitney, MPA

Microcosm Publishing
Portland, OR

QUIT YOUR DAY JOB WORKBOOK

Building the DIY Project, Life, and Business of Your Dreams

Part of the DIY Series

© Eleanor C. Whitney, 2020

This edition © Microcosm Publishing, 2020

First edition, first published September 2020

ISBN 9781621062578

This is Microcosm #618

Cover and design by Joe Biel with Jake English

For a catalog, write or visit:

Microcosm Publishing

2752 N Williams Ave.

Portland, OR 97227

503-799-2698

www.microcosmpublishing.com

These worksheets can be used on their own, or as a companion to **Quit Your Day Job** by Eleanor C. Whitney www.Microcosm.Pub/DayJob

These worksheets are free to reproduce but no more than two can be reproduced in a publication without expressed permission from the publisher. Find supplemental spreadsheets at www.Microcosm.Pub/QYDJ

To join the ranks of high-class stores that feature Microcosm titles, talk to your rep: In the U.S. **Como** (Atlantic), **Fujii** (Midwest), **Book Travelers West** (Pacific), **Turnaround** in Europe, **Manda/UTP** in Canada, **New South** in Australia, and **GPS** in Asia, India, Africa, and South America. We are sold in the gift market by **Gifts of Nature.**

Did you know that you can buy our books directly from us at sliding scale rates? Support a small, independent publisher and pay less than Amazon's price at www.Microcosm.Pub

Global labor conditions are bad, and our roots in industrial Cleveland in the 70s and 80s made us appreciate the need to treat workers right. Therefore, our books are MADE IN THE USA.

MICROCOSM · PUBLISHING

Microcosm Publishing is Portland's most diversified publishing house and distributor with a focus on the colorful, authentic, and empowering. Our books and zines have put your power in your hands since 1996, equipping readers to make positive changes in their lives and in the world around them. Microcosm emphasizes skill-building, showing hidden histories, and fostering creativity through challenging conventional publishing wisdom with books and bookettes about DIY skills, food, bicycling, gender, self-care, and social justice. What was once a distro and record label was started by Joe Biel in his bedroom and has become among the oldest independent publishing houses in Portland, OR. We are a politically moderate, centrist publisher in a world that has inched to the right for the past 80 years.

CONTENTS

REFLECT, REASSESS, AND STAY MOTIVATED 203

RECOGNIZING YOUR PROJECT'S LIFECYCLE: CONSIDERATIONS FOR ENDING OR CHANGING 209

INTRODUCTION

"**G**o DIY!" is still stenciled on the floor of my parents' basement in rural Maine. It is left behind from a silkscreen project I did in the late nineties while I was still in high school. I was creating patches to share my love of do it yourself culture with the world.

DIY or "Do It Yourself" is widely defined, but for the purposes of this book, it means taking initiative to independently create a project that is largely driven, and put together, by you. It means pursuing your dreams and creating projects that you are excited about while not waiting for permission from experts or traditional cultural gatekeepers like editors, publishers, record labels, galleries, curators, directors, or the companies they are tied to. "Do It Yourself" also involves a willingness to learn new skills and take risks to put yourself out there. Through embracing DIY, you are also embracing the opportunity to grow as a creative person.

While DIY means that you are the driving force behind your project, as my friend Amy Schroeder always said, "Do It Yourself does not mean do it alone." DIY projects thrive on community and collaboration. For motivation, collaboration, and accountability, enlist a few friends or neighbors who have similar visions to you, and make plans with them. This can also be a great way to get to know the people around you in new and different ways.

In addition to nurturing your relationship to others, DIY also means taking care of yourself, and learning to assert your boundaries and limits. Because your project relies on you, taking a DIY approach also means pursuing your project in an organized and financially sustainable manner. *Quit Your Day Job: The Workbook* will help you take the big leap to begin your project, focus your creative energy, and tackle the practical and logistical elements you need in order to build a sustainable, successful project. When you thrive, so does your project!

You probably picked up this book because you have a project that you are so excited to work on it keeps you up at night. You know that society needs to be changed and you have a way to change it. You've just been struck by inspiration or you have been nurturing a plan for a long time. Either way, you are ready to take action and make your vision a reality. You are ready to change the world with your project. When you start a Do It Yourself project, you empower yourself and take charge of your life by working to make something concrete from your creative vision. When you take on a Do It Yourself project, you bring an entrepreneurial, transformational spirit in your life.

A DIY project can take on any size or scope that you want. It could be a podcast that records the stories of local activists, a photography class for neighborhood teenagers who don't have access to art education at school, a daily diary comic that raises awareness about climate change that you share on social media, the debut album for your band, publishing a poetry chapbook and organizing a reading, setting up an online store for your pottery, aerobics classes for punks, a store and community gathering place that sells local, handmade goods, or anything that activates your creativity, values, and ambition.

In the over twenty years since I made that stencil, DIY culture has continued to impact and shape my life in ways I couldn't imagine. I began publishing zines and playing in bands, and the people I met in this subculture are still some of my closest friends. DIY introduced me to feminist organizing, the LGBTQ community, and anti-racist politics and helped me find my voice politically. Engaging in DIY projects that I cared about led me to two careers: one as educator, fundraiser, and business advisor in the arts, and the other as a marketer and community builder for tech startups and creative, innovative companies. As I've juggled my careers and creative projects, I realized the skills I gained from doing it myself could help other creative people bring their projects to life and build the jobs and lives they dream of.

One of the strengths of taking a DIY approach to a creative project or business idea is that you can start small and grow at a pace that feels sustainable and right for you. You have the power to define "success" on your own terms. Capitalist culture has a very narrow vision of success, and spreads the myth that success is only available to a few winners, and the rest of us are losers. Taking a DIY approach means defining success is up to you. Your success can nurture your creativity and give back to your community. Your success could get publicity for the artist collective you work with. Your success can make your political action group more accessible to anyone interested. The most important part is that you get to build a project that reflects your values and vision for the world.

From talking with hundreds of creative people over the years, and building my own creative projects, I've found the following ideas underpin most successful DIY projects, and they serve as the guiding principles of this workbook:

- Assess your skills and be honest about your strengths and weaknesses

- Cultivate a space, time and routine that maximizes your creativity

- Think of yourself, and your project, as a long term investment

- Value the DIY community

- Clearly define your goals and expectations when working with other people

- Communication creates healthy collaboration

- Good will is your most valuable asset

- Regularly assess your project and your feelings about it to decide when it's time to grow, pivot, or move on

- Be persistent and build the life that you dream of

Throughout this workbook you'll find exercises that help you define and refocus on your values and reflect on what success feels like for you personally. You'll also find quotes and insights from people who I interviewed for my book *Quit Your Day Job*, who have found success on their own terms. I want to share some of their wisdom to you to remind you that while your project is singular to you, the challenge and opportunity to bring your idea to life is shared. You are not alone!

The book is structured so each exercise and section builds on the one before it, and it will walk you through the basics of planning and goal setting; branding and marketing; budgeting, finances, and fundraising; how to think about business structure; building healthy work habits and a DIY life that supports your project; and the planning and preparation you need to undertake to make the leap to full time DIY.

You can use this workbook as a companion to my book *Quit Your Day Job*, which is filled with more useful information and practical advice from creative people, or as a stand alone workbook. It is a tool for you!

I suggest you start with the "Plan Your Dream Project" section. That section will enable you to articulate a clear idea of your project, its mission, and vision, and you will be ready to identify and take the steps you need to grow! After starting here, you may find it helpful to skip around to the sections that feel the most urgent or relevant to your project—that's fine, the goal of this workbook is to make it your own!

I've compiled some sample documents to help you with budgeting and planning. You can find them at http://microcosm.pub/qydj

I encourage you to try exercises that feel outside of your comfort zone, whether that be branding, budgeting, or building a clear, communicative relationship with a project collaborator. It is in these moments of stretching ourselves to try something new that we grow the most and give our projects, and ourselves, what they need to find the next level of success.

Building your dream project, and life, is no small feat, but the great part of DIY is that you can start right here, right now, where you are and trust you are already enough to get there. Ready? Let's get growing.

PLAN YOUR DREAM PROJECT

This chapter will help you take the big leap to begin your project from scratch and focus your creative energy. It will guide you through the process of making a mission and vision statement, defining goals and action steps, creating a project timeline, and setting project deadlines. When you have a mission, goals and a timeline for your project, you lay the groundwork for success and create a firm foundation on which to grow.

Choose the Right Project for Right Now

As dynamic, complex, creative people we often have many different ideas. This is exciting and inspiring, but can also prevent us from giving a project the time, energy, and resources it needs to thrive. Big ideas benefit from consistent focus. If you feel overwhelmed and unsure what idea to choose, this exercise can help you decide which one of your ideas to begin to actualize now.

List your project ideas here:

1.

2.

3.

4.

5.

For each idea answer the following questions:

Idea #1

I'm excited about this idea because . . .

This idea will help me realize my creative goals by . . .

The resources and skills I need to realize this idea are . . .

Now is a good time to bring this idea to life because . . .

How much time do I think I will need to actualize this idea?

On a scale of 1 to 5, 5 being the highest, how excited am I about this idea?

Idea #2

I'm excited about this idea because . . .

This idea will help me realize my creative goals by . . .

The resources and skills I need to realize this idea are . . .

Now is a good time to bring this idea to life because . . .

How much time do I think I will need to actualize this idea?

On a scale of 1 to 5, 5 being the highest, how excited am I about this idea?

Idea #3

I'm excited about this idea because . . .

This idea will help me realize my creative goals by . . .

The resources and skills I have to realize this idea are . . .

Now is a good time to bring this idea to life because . . .

How much time do I think I will need to actualize this idea?

On a scale of 1 to 5, 5 being the highest, how excited am I about this idea?

Idea #4

I'm excited about this idea because . . .

This idea will help me realize my creative goals by . . .

The resources and skills I have to realize this idea are . . .

Now is a good time to bring this idea to life because . . .

How much time do I think I will need to actualize this idea?

On a scale of 1 to 5, 5 being the highest, how excited am I about this idea?

Idea #5

I'm excited about this idea because . . .

This idea will help me realize my creative goals by . . .

The resources and skills I have to realize this idea are . . .

Now is a good time to bring this idea to life because . . .

How much time do I think I will need to actualize this idea?

On a scale of 1 to 5, 5 being the highest, how excited am I about this idea?

Read back through your answers and reflect on them. Which idea are you most excited about? Which one helps you realize your goals? Which one is the most possible given your skills, resources, and time commitments? You might choose to prioritize the most realistic idea, or you might choose the most ostentatious one. Only you can know what the right idea is for you right now, but remember, no idea is lost. You can always record your ideas to come back to later.

Clarify Your Project: Start Now, Where You Are

Moving a project from idea to reality is exciting and can be daunting. Once you've chosen a project to focus on, take advantage of the inspiration and energy you feel to move that new idea forward. Trust that you already have the capabilities within you that you need to bring your project to life.

It's always intimidating to get started, but these simple questions will help you narrow down the focus of your project. Take time to write down your answers to each. To start, ask yourself a few simple questions.

Describe your project in one sentence:

While the idea of describing your project clearly and concisely may sound like a simple place to start, it is one of the most challenging parts of the process. When you understand deeply and clearly what you will create you can begin your project with focus and determination.

Why are you passionate about this project?

For example, how does this project relate to your personal goals, values, and sense of yourself and what you love?

What motivates you to work on it?

Examples include making extra income, learning a new skill, contributing to your community, or sharing your passion with others.

Is it a brand new project or have you been working on it for a long time?

If it's a new project, why is now a good time to start?

If you've been working on it for a long time, how and why and are ready to expand or take it in a new direction?

What do you hope to achieve with this project?

For example:

A profitable business within one year.

Enough extra income to pay off my student loans.

A business that allows me to donate my profits to support a charity or community organization I care about.

To be a recognized, trusted expert in my field.

A community gathering place/event for my community [define them]

What details do you know already about your project?

Timing, resources you have or need, demand for what you are offering, common challenges, or specific opportunities in your area? List them here:

What details about your project are you still unsure or curious about?

How much do you know about the skills and knowledge your project requires? *Are you a complete beginner? An expert? Somewhere in the middle? How will you go about learning what you need to know?*

Do you have a community of friends and family that know about, and support, your project? *List specific supporters and how they may be able to support you here.*

Envision Success

Ask yourself: what do you want to achieve with your project? Engage your imagination and think big. Daydream!

In this section, you'll imagine what success looks and feels like and record this vision in a way you can easily revisit. Everyone visions and learns in different ways, so you can choose from the exercises below for the ones that work best. I also encourage you to take risks. For example, I was skeptical of vision boarding until I tried it and now it's a regular part of my creative process.

Success daydream / meditation

Set aside half an hour or more and settle into a quiet place, either sitting or lying down comfortably (but not so comfortable you'll fall asleep!).

- Close your eyes or keep them open but softly focused.

- Take deep breaths to center yourself.

- Remember, during this process, nothing is "right" or "wrong"—it's about letting your mind wander enough so that you can connect with your deeper visions and desires.

- Once you feel centered and relaxed, imagine that your project is finished and it has been successful.

- What have you created?

- Imagine the "final product"—if it's a tangible object, what does it feel like to hold it in your hands? What materials is it made out of?

- What does it look like?

- If it's an event or a space, how is it decorated?

- Who is in the space with you?

- What kind of feedback are you receiving about your project?

- What are people saying to you?

- How do you feel in your body?

Sit with these visions for as long as you like and then take time to write them down here, or in a journal, sketch them out, or just write key words on sticky notes or note cards—whatever will enable you to easily revisit and recall this vision of success.

For example, if you want to play in a band, picture what success for your band means. Imagine that you have recorded an album that is well received and have gone on tour. What does your record cover look like? Where are the reviews published and what do the reviews say? Who is coming to your shows? What do they tell you after you play? What kind of venues are you playing? How do you get from show to show? What is the relationship like with your other bandmates? How does it feel to be on stage? How do you feel overall about the project?

Create a vision board

A vision board is a collage of images that represents your vision for success in an abstract, aspirational manner. I find that creating a vision board is the most fun when you create a physical board by cutting images from magazines or other visual material, arranging them on a piece of posterboard, and sticking them down with a glue stick. It doesn't need to be a great work of art, just a piece that speaks to you!

I have an annual tradition of creating a yearly vision board at the start of the new year. It helps me clarify not only what I want to do and achieve, but also how I want to feel. At the end of the year, I reflect back and feel amazed with how often my visions come to life!

If cutting and pasting isn't your thing, you can also create a digital vision board using Pinterest, Tumblr, or an app to collect inspiring images from the internet.

Vision board directions:
This can be a fun activity to do with friends who are also working on creative projects or goals.

Materials needed: Old magazines, poster board (as small or big as you feel comfortable, I find legal or letter size works great), scissors, glue stick, mod podge (optional), brush (optional), washi tape (optional).

- Clarify what you are creating your vision board for—for example, to capture your vision of success for your project overall or to imagine a specific phase in the project

- Give yourself and hour or two to create your vision board—you want to relax and work without stress or time pressure

- Look through the magazines and pull out any images, words, or phrases that speak to you

- Don't think too hard about what you are choosing—let your intuition guide you

- As you look for images you might find you are getting more specific about what you are looking for

- Once you feel you have a nice pile of images and words assembled, sort through them and edit out any that feel too repetitive or like they no longer speak to you

- Arrange your images on your poster board and trim them so they fit together nicely and create an overall image that you like

- Glue the images down with a glue stick

- Coat the completed collage with a thin coat of Mod Podge to tie it all together and to protect it

- Once the Mod Podge has dried, create a frame for the board or accent it with decorative washi tape

- Once your board is complete, reflect on what you have created in the space below—how does it represent your vision of success?

- Display your finished board above your mirror, dresser, or desk—anywhere you can look at it often to feel inspired

- Take a picture of your vision board and use it as your wallpaper or lock screen on your phone so it can give you a small reminder of your goals each time you pick up your phone

How does your vision board reflect how success will look and feel?

Summarize your vision of success

Now that you've taken time to visualize success and define what it means to you, it can be helpful to distill that vision into a single sentence or phrase. When you are specific about your vision you will have a clear idea of the steps you need to take to actualize it.

Complete the sentence:

I will have succeeded when…

From a broad vision of success like this you can then start to focus on creating a mission statement and goals that will guide you through the creative process.

Clarify Your Core Values

Your values are what guide and motivate you. When you clarify the values that drive you it can be easier to make decisions about what is right for your project.

Write down all of the values you can think of that help guide your life:

Think about past creative projects, what you value in relationships to people, your political beliefs and activism, the communities that you are part of, and the kinds of work you do and do not take on.

From that list, identify 6 to 8 that you feel are the most important, powerful, or relevant to you right now that feel like your personal "North Star:"

1.

2.

3.

4.

5.

6.

7.

8.

How can your project embody or reflect those values?:

Craft Your Mission and Vision Statements

Use your core values and vision of success as a guide to craft your mission and vision statements. These statements will ground and guide your project. They are something to come back to when you need a reminder as to why you are doing a project or to guage if a decision or opportunity is a good fit for you and your project.

A mission statement is a clear, to-the-point statement that helps define and guide a company, organization or project. It sums up in a few sentences what the project aims to achieve, who they serve, and outlines in the broadest terms how they will accomplish their goals.

A vision statement captures the broad vision of success and social impact that a company, organization, or project will have. It captures your hopes and dreams, summarizes the larger problem you are trying to solve, and imagines the change that you are trying to inspire.

Drafting and crafting a mission and vision statements is a process. Before you write your mission statement look at the mission statements for organizations you admire. Do they seem understandable or off the mark given what you know about that organization?

When you have a draft of your mission statement read it out loud. Make sure the language flows and that you have accurately captured your vision. Show a draft of your mission statement to friends and ask for their feedback. Keep revising your mission and vision statements until it fully encompasses what you hope to achieve.

Write your mission statement

Your mission statement should be concise, memorable, far-reaching, and practical. It articulates the purpose of your project: what you want to achieve, why you are doing it, and how. Your mission statement should give you a rush of inspiration and purpose each time you read it.

Describe your project in 10 seconds. Write it down:

Describe your project in 30 seconds. Write it down:

In one sentence what does or will your project do?

List three core values that drive your project:

1.

2.

3.

Revisit your vision of success. Now shape it all together into a paragraph:

That's your mission statement!

Feeling stuck? Try this mission statement framework to create a first draft and then revise and expand from there.

Write your vision statement

Your vision statement captures what you aspire to be or have accomplished when your mission is achieved. It builds upon your core values and your vision of success. It should feel lofty—a vision statement is aspirational.

To write it, revisit your motivation for this project and your core values. Respond to these prompts to help write a first draft of your vision statement:

Name of company / project will help achieve a world with / without (choose one):

Name of company / project believes that:

Name of company /project will contribute to:

Name of company /project envisions:

From these answers, choose what you feel resonates the most for you and write your vision statement:

Type vision and mission statements and print them out where you can look at them constantly—perhaps display them with your vision board or keep them as wallpaper or sticky notes on your computer desktop.

Resource Assessment

Taking stock of the resources you have and need will help you plan and budget for your project. For example, you might need to create project goals around identifying and securing additional resources, or work in time for fundraising. We'll cover budgeting in detail later in this workbook, but this brainstorm will help you understand what you need, what you have, and what you need to source elsewhere.

Resources can mean money, time, space, specific skills, support, and events. Think as broadly as possible as you brainstorm below:

Resources I have personally:

Resources available to me in my community:

Resources I need:

Resources I still need to figure out how to get:

Resources I can offer others:

Define Your Goals

Setting goals makes your mission statement concrete. Goals are precise and result-oriented statements about what you will achieve. Goals can be both practical and audacious, but the goals you set for your project should inspire you to action.

To start out, set three to four big goals. A limited number of goals makes your project more manageable; set too many goals, and you'll get your objectives confused. Make each goal distinct, and ensure that each one relates back to your mission statement and your vision of success. You can set goals that are very simple, but dare to push yourself. As you achieve your goals, you'll set new ones.

Write goals that start with action verbs, which make you feel motivated, focused, and excited to achieve them.

A good guideline for goals is to keep them SMART:

- Specific

- Measurable

- Action-oriented

- Realistic

- Time-bound

Write 3 to 4 big goals using the "goal mad lib" below to help create SMART goals.

Goal mad lib:

_____   _____   _____
[action verb]   [quantifiable task accomplished]   [time when the task will be

_____
accomplished]

For example, if you are in a band: "Book and play six shows by the end of the year"

Big goals:

1.

2.

3.

4.

Create Action Steps to Support Your Goals

Once you have your big goals defined, it's time to get practical. Breaking each of your big goals into specific action steps will help you work towards them. To do this ask yourself, "What needs to be done to accomplish my goal?" Write all of these tasks down. Then organize these tasks into a list in the order they need to be accomplished. As you work on your project this order may change and you may add and subtract tasks, but having a list of bite-sized tasks will enable you to work methodically towards your big goal.

For example, continuing the big goal from the last activity, another one of your goals could be to book and play six shows by the end of the year, one of your goals is to identify which venues you want to play. An action step could be to make a list of all the venues in town that book similar bands as yours, and/or reach out to the venues and inquire about booking. These smaller, action oriented steps act like mile markers along the roadmap of success. They keep your project on track and give you a sense of accomplishment and motivation when you achieve them. Depending on the size and complexity of your big goals you might need to break your action steps into still smaller subtasks.

Create action steps

Break each of your goals into specific action steps that will help you achieve them. List your goal and then all all of the tasks you can think of that need to be completed in order to accomplish that goal (think big and small!):

From this list, match at least three of your action steps to each of your goals. To keep your goals time-bound, set an approximate date by which you will accomplish each of these action steps.

Example:
Goal 1: Book and play six shows by the end of the year

Action step 1: Make a list of venues that play bands similar to yours

Specific tasks: Use Google Maps and venue websites to gauge what kind of bands, and what size bands, play at venues around town

Action step 2: Determine which venues seem like the best fit

Specific tasks: Consult with bandmates about which venues seem like they will support your band, and make a decision all together to contact a handful of venues

Action step 3: Call or email the venue's booking agents and inquire about booking fees, availabilities, and the possibility of booking multiple dates.

Use the space below to create action steps to move you towards your goals.

Goal 1:

Action step 1:

Specific tasks:

Deadline:

Action step 2:

Specific tasks:

Deadline:

Action step 3:

Specific tasks:

Deadline:

Goal 2:

Action step 1:

Specific tasks:

Deadline:

Action step 2:

Specific tasks:

Deadline:

Action step 3:

Specific tasks:

Deadline:

Goal 3:

Action step 1:

Specific tasks:

Deadline:

Action step 2:

Specific tasks:

Deadline:

Action step 3:

Specific tasks:

Deadline:

Project Timeline

When do you want to achieve your ultimate goal? How long will your action steps and supporting tasks take to complete? A timeline will guide you and enable you to keep your project on track. It is an essential tool when you are balancing your project with the rest of your life.

When you are working out your timeline, give yourself the time you need to achieve your goals. Account for other activities and events in your life. Are you graduating from school or taking a major trip? Do you have a job that gets busy during a certain time of year? Be honest about your other time commitments. Many of us have what is called "optimism bias" when it comes to completing tasks because we think everything will go smoothly and be completed in the shortest time possible without interruption. When you are realistic about your timeline, you avoid getting discouraged. Give yourself enough time to complete your project, considering setbacks, but be sure that your deadlines are tight enough that they keep you motivated.

Storyboard your timeline

If you are a visual thinker, or just need another way to work out and reinforce your timeline and deadlines, try illustrating it like a storyboard. Make a sketch for each task you need to complete in the boxes on the next page. You can cross off the boxes as you complete the different tasks in order to get a sense of progress and momentum.

Whether you are using a calendar, an online project tracker, a storyboard, or a list, make sure you can access them whenever you need to hold yourself accountable

Make a workback timeline

Sometimes, it is most helpful to start with the end product or date in mind and work backwards from there. In the tables on pages 43-45, fill in the blocks of time you expect each part of the project to take. You may find as you make it that supporting steps will take longer than you thought and you'll have to move the deadline out. After creating this in the workbook you may want to format in a spreadsheet, calendar, or task manager like Trello or Airtable. Or you can make a copy of the spreadsheet at http://microcosm.pub/qydj to use with your

Storyboard Exercise

Sketch Task 1

Sketch Task 2

Sketch Task 3

Project Launch/Kick Off

Workback Timeline Exercise
(Example of a filled out workback timeline)

	Week 1	Week 2	Week 3	Week 4	Week 5	Week 6
Market Research						
Fundraising						

Completion/Launch date

Research/Planning/Preparation

	Week 1	Week 2	Week 3	Week 4	Week 5	Week 6
Task 1						
Task 2						
Task 3						

Project Launch/Kick Off

	Week 1	Week 2	Week 3	Week 4	Week 5	Week 6
Task 1						
Task 2						
Task 3						

Project Production

	Week 1	Week 2	Week 3	Week 4	Week 5	Week 6
Task 1						
Task 2						
Task 3						

([you may need to break this part up into different sub-stages])

Project Review/Refinement

	Week 1	Week 2	Week 3	Week 4	Week 5	Week 6
Task 1						
Task 2						
Task 3						

Project Finishing

	Week 1	Week 2	Week 3	Week 4	Week 5	Week 6
Task 1						
Task 2						
Task 3						

Post-launch

	Week 1	Week 2	Week 3	Week 4	Week 5	Week 6
Task 1						
Task 2						
Task 3						

Reflection/Review/Next Stage Planning

	Week 1	Week 2	Week 3	Week 4	Week 5	Week 6
Task 1						
Task 2						
Task 3						

own information. and track progress. Revise your timeline as you achieve your intermediate goals and get a better sense of how long the different elements of your project will take.

When the big ideas for a project are clear and you spend time defining a mission, setting goals and action steps, and making a timeline, you will be prepared to tackle the practical and logistical aspects of your project with focus and grace. When you have these elements in place, you'll be well situated to get started.

Chapter One Checklist

- ○ Narrow down your ideas and refine potential projects

- ○ Envision success using a success meditation, vision board, and other reflective tools

- ○ Clarify the core values that give your project purpose and direction

- ○ Curate your mission and vision statements, respectively, to begin sharing your intentions with the world in a concise, articulate manner

- ○ Assess the resources you need, have, do and do not have access to, and how to get them

- ○ Define your goals, and break them down into actionable, approachable steps

- ○ Draft a working timeline aimed at keeping your work balanced with your personal endeavors

GIVE YOUR PROJECT AN IDENTITY

BRANDING BASICS

B efore you share your project with the world, it needs a well defined audience and identity. Having both of these will make it easier to build a website, launch social media accounts, create a fundraising campaign, or launch a marketing initiative. Even if your project is as simple as offering your services, like writing, photography, or tarot readings to your community, clarifying your audience and your project identity will help you when it's time to get the word out.

Market Research

Understanding your market means understanding what you are offering and to whom, and who else is offering similar products or services. While some companies and business owners might look at market research as getting insight into their "competition," instead, think of your research as a way to better understand your audience and your community. This will help you figure how you could best serve them and identify potential collaborators, like-minded people, and businesses to support.

Understand your project

Write down answers to the following questions below.

Are you selling a product and need customers?

Are your customers going to be individuals or other businesses organizations?

Are you performing or presenting and need audience members?

Are you building a public movement or campaign and need volunteers and public supporters?

Are you taking on a large-scale project where you will need partners, collaborators, or collective members to realize it?

Understand your community or market

Now that you have defined what you are offering and to whom, spend some time understanding the community in which your project or business will exist.

List five other projects or businesses that are similar to yours:

1.

2.

3.

4.

5.

For each business or project, list three similarities to your project and three differences.

Business #1

Similarities:

1.

2.

3.

Differences:

1.

2.

3.

Business #2

Similarities:

1.

2.

3.

Differences:

1

2.

3.

Business #3

Similarities:

1.

2.

3.

Differences:

1.

2.

3.

Business #4

Similarities:

1.

2.

3.

Differences:

1.

2.

3.

Business #5

Similarities:

1.

2.

3.

Differences:

1.

2.

3.

Reflect on the above and summarize in 2 to 3 sentences what makes your project or business different from others like it:

Identify your target audience

When you have a better idea about the context in which your project exists, now think about the specific audience you want to reach. You might think of these people as your "dream customer," "target market," or simply your peers. They are the people who will benefit from knowing about your project, product, or business and be your customers, advocates, and supporters. These people can help you spread the word and give you feedback so you can continue to refine your project and grow.

When thinking about your "target audience" you want to get specific as possible. It's important to avoid making assumptions, or dealing in stereotypes, when it comes to groups of people, but you do want to understand the different groups of people who you want to serve.

Take as much time as you need to answer the questions below:

Who wants or needs your product, project or service?

Who are the people who are already connected to your project? List them here:

For example, you may already be making a zine, playing in a band, or part of a collective or community organized around your interest.

Does the audience that you imagine for your project resemble this group of people you are already connected to or will you need to expand who you reach in order to achieve the success you dream of?

Who are the specific people that you dream of using your product, project or service? List them here:

To understand your target audience answer the following questions:

How old are they?

What education level do they have?

Where do they live?

What is their job?

How much money do they make (approximately)?

What do they like to do?

Where do they get their news and information?

What do they do for fun? What are their interests?

What other organizations and networks of people are interested in the ideas and issues that drive your project? List them here:

Create "personas" for your customers

As you do this exercise, you may have found that your idea, project, or business could appeal to multiple types of people. This is great! Look at your answers above and create three distinct characters that personify your ideal customers. Give them a name, profession, and hobbies, think about where they live and what their house or apartment is like. Giving your potential community members or customers specific identities can help guide you about how they might relate to your work.

Persona 1:

Name:

Age:

Profession:

Education:

Location, city, state, neighborhood, type of house:

Interests and hobbies:

Pets, family members, housemates:

Why are they interested in your project? How does your project relate to who they are?

Persona 2:

Name:

Age:

Profession:

Education:

Location, city, state, neighborhood, type of house:

Interests and hobbies:

Pets, family members, housemates:

Why are they interested in your project? How does your project relate to who they are?

Persona 3:

Name:

Age:

Profession:

Education:

Location, city, state, neighborhood, type of house:

Interests and hobbies:

Pets, family members, housemates:

Why are they interested in your project? How does your project relate to who they are?

Get to Know Your Brand

Your brand is how your project or business is presented to your ideal customers and community. By making conscious, thoughtful decisions about how your project is presented to the world, you empower yourself to take control of your image and help guide how your project is received.

Branding goes beyond a logo and visual identity for your project or business, though these are important elements for your brand. Once you have a clear idea of what qualities you want your brand to embody you can work with a designer (or design yourself) a visual identity for your project.

How do you want to be known? What do you want to be known for? When you brand yourself, you decide!

Revisit your core values. How does your project or business embody those values?

Make a list of keywords that you want associated with your project. Now choose the three strongest, most distinct words that best capture your project:

List all of the personality attributes that you want associated with your brand. Now choose the three strongest, most distinct personalities that best capture your project.

Make a list of people, either who you know personally or public figures, who embody your brand's personality:

Complete the sentence: I want to be known for . . .

What would your project or business eat for breakfast?

If your project or business was throwing a party, what would it be like? What food would be served, where would it be, what would the decorations be like, who would be invited?

List three inspirations (people, places, objects, ideas, social movements, etc.) for your brand:

How do you want your project or business to make your customers or community feel? What about it makes your audience want to get involved?

To capture the feeling of your brand visually, you might want to make a specific vision board or collage specific to your brand.

Understanding your market, community, the audience you want to reach with your project, and who you are as a brand will lay the foundation for your marketing, outreach, fundraising, community building, and overall sharing your project with the world.

Chapter Two Checklist

Conduct market research to get a sense of who, what, when, where and why your project has something to offer the world:

○   Identify your target audience

○   Flesh out the characteristics that make your audience specific

○   Create personas for your customers

Brand yourself as a means of communicating your core values and intentions to your audience:

○   Consider how your brand will reflect your core values

○   Make a list of words you want associated with your brand

○   Create a brand vision board

SPREADING THE WORD AND TELLING THE WORLD

MARKETING AND COMMUNITY BUILDING BASICS

While the word "marketing" can sound very corporate, at the base of any genuine marketing effort is the desire to connect with people whose interests match up with yours and build a community around that shared interest. The core of marketing is sharing what you do with people who have a shared interest and could benefit from your project.

Marketing is not only telling people about your project and how it can benefit them, but also listening to the needs, hopes and passions of those who are interested in your project. Only by learning from and with your community can you get perspective on how you should present your intentions to reach the widest and most interested audience possible.

"Marketing" in the broadest sense of the term includes anything that helps inform the world about your project: a website, email newsletters, social media presence, and press or "earned" media coverage. Like any phase of your project, it starts with a strong plan and healthy community relationships.

Create a Marketing Campaign Creative Brief

A marketing campaign is all the coordinated efforts you make to share your project with the world. A "creative brief" is an overview of the goals of your campaign and every tactic that you use to support and realize those goals. If you were to work with a marketing agency or PR representative, you would create a "brief" at the beginning of your relationship to clarify expectations and what you hope to achieve.

From a DIY perspective, having a campaign brief helps you get organized even if you are responsible for realizing each element of the campaign yourself. You can use this brief to define how you will market your project overall, or for specific initiatives, such as a new single for your band or a new issue of your comic zine.

Use this template below to put together your creative brief:

Project name:

Project leader:

Other stakeholders (people) involved and specific role:

Summarize target audience:

What does success look like? How will it be measured?

Timeline:

Deliverables:
What do you need to create for this project to be successful, ex. Website, printed brochure, press release, . . .

What channels will you be using to promote this campaign/your project:
Ex. Email, social media, in-person event (which might require its own creative brief), . . .

What assets do you need to create to support this campaign?
Ex. images for social media, photography, blog post, email, new web page

Press outreach: What media outlets do you plan to pitch to?

Key messages in order of priority:

- Headline Message:

- Message #1:

- Message #2:

- Message #3:

Call to action:

What will your campaign be asking those who interact with it to do? For example, buy your new book, subscribe to your podcast, sign up for your workshop

Other notes:

Next steps:

Develop Your Pitch

Remember your project's goals and mission statement? It's time to revisit them to craft your pitch for outreach. You will use this pitch in your printed and online materials, press releases, emails, and calls to people you want to collaborate with, as well as any time you talk about your project in casual conversation.

Your pitch should include:

- The who, what, where, when and why of your project

- A catchy, memorable description, or "tagline" for your project

- Basic information about who you are

Your pitch should reflect the personality and message that you have decided on for your brand. Is it friendly and welcoming? Avant garde and intriguing? Ensure that it is consistent with the image you want to reflect.

Greta Gertler, a musician who also does public relations for other musicians, emphasizes the personal behind the pitch, "The story of what you are doing is important. It is not just that your project is really great, but that you are sharing a story behind it. People are bombarded with inputs and you want your story to stand out."

Describe your project in one paragraph:
Refer to your mission and vision statements, values, and brand exercise.

Shorten your description to 1 - 2 sentences.
This is sometimes known as an "elevator pitch"—if you are in an elevator with someone and you have 30 seconds to tell them about what you are working on what will you say?

If you are stuck, try these examples to get started:

_____ is a _____ _____ that enables/creates (choose one)
[Name of project]   [adjective]   [description]

people to _____. It will be launching/released/coming out
[summary of value here]

_____ .
[date]

I am a_____ who creates_____
[description of what you do, ex. illustrator]   [description of

_____ for _____ in order to_____ .
the type of work that you make]   [audience]   [benefit for audience]

Write 3 to 4 versions of your pitch and share it with friends for feedback. What resonates with them most? Why?

Once you have your pitch, practice saying it aloud.

How to Reach Out, Talk about Your Project, and Grow Your Community

Networking is the basis of the do-it-yourself community and what makes the DIY community so special. It also is an important strategy for spreading the word about your project that goes deeper than traditional marketing. When you develop an outreach strategy, you identify organizations or individuals who could have a special interest in your project and an unique angle to support you and reach out to them individually before you launch a large-scale marketing campaign.

Forge genuine connections

Define and identify with whom you would like to connect for your project.

Reflect on the following questions:

Are there other creative people or organizations you want to collaborate with?

What do you need from community members? *Examples include advice, collaboration, reaching a similar audience, help expanding your network as a new member of the community*

What could you offer them in return?

What are your common or overlapping interests?

Reaching out to individuals one-on-one through email, a letter, or in person is a great way to cultivate a relationship and ask for their support. Successful outreach requires determining who is the right person to contact, and reaching out to them specifically, especially in the case of an organization. Once you have identified who that person is, pick up the phone or write a concise, polite, personal email.

Structure your outreach

When you reach out you are offering potential supporters compelling reasons to get involved in an exciting, creative project that will affect positive cultural change and get to know you as an interesting, dynamic, creative person. Creative people sometimes fear that asking for support can be interpreted as an act of desperation, but if you are clear about the project's goals and why their support is needed and appreciated, you can ask with confidence. The more secure and personal you are, the more likely people will be drawn into your project.

For help in writing an outreach email or crafting a script, refer to the "Develop your pitch" section above.

Key elements to an engaging outreach conversation:

- Introduce yourself

- Keep a positive, upbeat tone

- Be concise

- Summarize your project

- Explain why you are contacting them and propose how you could work together

- Give them a reason to work with you

- Let them know how their involvement could benefit you and/or the project

- Make a specific ask for support, such as a coffee meeting or attending an event you are organizing

- Invite them to discuss further or to ask questions

- Thank them for their time and consideration

Above all, let your passion and dedication show through and be respectful of your potential supporters' time and opinions.

If you don't hear back right away, follow up after about a week. People are busy, but it helps to be persistent without bombarding them with communication.

Have backups, too. Not everyone will be able to help you and you want to keep your options open.

Community building is key when conducting outreach. Outreach opens communication and offers you a chance to receive feedback and exchange ideas with those you contact. Through outreach you develop relationships with peers, supporters, and advocates who can support you throughout the life of your project.

Your Online Presence

A website is your online home and your opportunity to share all the information your audience needs to understand you and your project. You need to create your website before you begin major outreach. It need not be fancy, but should clearly reflect your brand, highlight the name of your project and where it is headed, and contain basic information about who you are and how to contact you.

A good, clean, functional website can be affordable. There are many website and blog services that offer templates where you can plug in your information and customize to your heart's content. Others offer template websites for specific disciplines, such as visual artists, musicians, or small business owners.

Many template websites offer a range of options, which vary in price depending on things like storage space and whether you want a custom URL. Before you start building your website, assess what you need it to do for your project:

Website Checklist

Check all that apply. I need to use my website to:

- ○ Build my network
  - ○ Contact form
  - ○ Newsletter signup
  - ○ Link and highlight social media accounts
- ○ Engage my community
  - ○ Host a blog
  - ○ Host a podcast

- Provide opportunity for comments or interactions between visitors, such as a connection to join a Google Group or Slack team
- Calendar or list of upcoming events or tour dates
- Sell tickets for events
- Elevate my reputation or brand
  - Appealing look and user experience
  - High-quality images
  - Uses current technology
  - Easy to update the content, such as images and text
  - Descriptive, easy-to-remember and type domain name that relates to your project
- Sell products
  - Attractive and easy-to-use product listings
  - Easy to group products into categories
  - Secure payment processing
  - Add shipping options
  - Wholesale and retail sales capability
- Advertise/sell services
  - Display resume/CV
  - Display testimonials or reviews
  - Include examples of past projects
- Share creative work
  - Visual galleries for photography or other visual art
  - Video embedding or hosting
  - Music/audio embedding or hosting
- Scale and grow your project
  - Will this website and host support a greater range of projects and/or more complex functionality as my project matures?

Basic website functionality checklist:

- ◯ Simple navigation
- ◯ Readable fonts
- ◯ High contrast colors (avoid light text on a light background)
- ◯ ADA compliant
- ◯ Include basic information about you and your project such as:
  - ◯ Description
  - ◯ Your bio or resume
  - ◯ Upcoming events
  - ◯ How to order goods you have for sale
  - ◯ Contact information
- ◯ Links to your social media
- ◯ Ensure your website loads and reads easily on multiple browsers and operating systems
- ◯ Tag your site with keywords so that it comes up in searches
- ◯ Keep information up-to-date

Create an Email Newsletter

Sending regular email newsletters is a very effective way to build, and connect directly, with your community of supporters, customers, and peers. They are more targeted than social media, and can speak directly to your specific audience. As social media platforms get more cluttered with bots, paid advertising, and algorithms that can make which posts show up in peoples' feeds inconsistent, email newsletters have become a more popular way of maintaining a more authentic and intimate connection with community members.

You can collect email addresses from supporters at events and customers who buy products on your website, make a post on your social media platforms encouraging your followers to sign up, and invite friends you already email regularly to subscribe. Ensure that you have explicit permission to email the people on your list.

There are many free email services out there that help you build and maintain lists and send beautiful emails.

Before launching an email newsletter, reflect on the following questions:

What are three goals of my email newsletter:

1.

2.

3.

What will you call your newsletter?

Who is the audience?

How often do I plan to send it out?

What kind of information will it include?

What strategies will you utilize to publicize, generate excitement about, and encourage your community to sign up to receive the newsletter?

Quick tips for effective email newsletters

- Keep it concise: Readers' time and attention is extremely precious

- Clearly state what your project offers in each newsletter

- Explicitly tell readers what you want them to do after reading:

  - Include links and "calls to action"

- Send yourself a test email and test all your links

- Send Tuesday through Friday, between 10 am and 2pm if possible (this might be hard if your readers are spread across many time zones)

  - This has been shown to be the most effective time to send emails

- Test what formats work best for your audience

  - They may prefer shorter emails with one focus or a more substantial newsletter

  - You can test this by asking your readers to send feedback, or experimenting with formats, and see what generates higher open rates

- Look at open rates and click rates

  - What type of content is your audience interacting with the most?

Depending on the goals of your newsletter, you may want to take a more personal approach and write it like an actual letter, or use it to list news highlights and upcoming events, like a more traditional newsletter. Use the templates below to help plan. Remember, depending on what you want to share, you can always switch up the format!

Sample "letter style" newsletter template:

Subject line: [About 50 characters or less] *Make it catchy and relevant*

Preview text: [40 to 130 characters] *Entice readers, ask a question, or highlight what's in your email*

Body Text: [3 - 4 short paragraphs]

Salutation:

Sample email newsletter template:

Subject line: [About 50 characters or less] *Make it catchy and relevant*

Preview text: [40 to 130 characters] *Entice readers, ask a question, or highlight what's in your email*

Headline:

Intro: *1 paragraph summarizing what's in the email*

Feature #1 headline:

Feature #1 image:

Feature #1 one-sentence description:

Feature #1 link/call to action:

Feature #2 headline:

Feature #2 image:

Feature #2 one-sentence description:

Feature #2 link/call to action:

Feature #3 headline:

Feature #3 image:

Feature #3 one-sentence description:

Feature #3 link/call to action:

Your Presence on Social Media

Social media platforms enable you to build a whole world around your project, connect with and share it with your communities, and find like-minded people. Social media feels personal and immediate. It is an opportunity for your audience to get a behind-the-scenes look at your project and get to know you better.

As you plan how you will represent your project on social media, remember: relationships are still relationships. Think of participating in social media as a conversation that is constantly evolving. When posting, privilege authentic connection and sincere sharing over quick snark: your online reputation is a big part of how your brand, and you, are known.

The world of social media changes fast and new platforms are launching constantly. For those new to social media, or who are only familiar with a few sites, it can feel overwhelming to take on yet another platform. In addition, social media can be all consuming if you aren't careful to set clear goals and boundaries for it. While it can feel frighteningly easy to compare yourself to others and their appearance of success, you don't know what's really happening unless they share their actual sales numbers with you. Developing a social media strategy can help keep you focused as you navigate the social media landscape. Proactively decide on which platforms to engage and how you want to share your project with your community. Don't be afraid to start small, and focus on what you already know. A strategy can also help keep you focused on what is working for you and driving success, whether that's sales, sign-ups or other types of engagement in your project.

Social media guidelines

- Choose the platform(s) that you will regularly update and feel comfortable using

- Research which platforms your audience is using and be active on those

- Choose one platform over another based on your brand identity and the goals of your project

- Diversify your social media presence across several platforms so you are not overly dependent on one if the technology or algorithm changes

- Update your profile and post regularly

- Ensure that the posts on your social media are consistent with your brand

- Respond to and interact with others

- Promote others' projects and share resources

- Know the popular social media influencers in your field

- Stay on top of trends in your field and new developments in technology

- Regularly assess whether your social media platforms, and strategy, are benefitting your project and serving your wider goals

The following exercises will enable you to plan a sustainable social media strategy and create a social media presence that is a complement to the vision, goals, and values for your project.

Choose the right platforms for your project

To choose the right platforms for your project, research and make notes about the following:

Investigate popular platforms: how are people in your community and people who inspire you using these platforms?

What type of content are they posting?

Are they selling products on these platforms?

Do they have a personal or a business account, or both?

What conversations are they having?

Who is responding to their posts? In which ways?

Use the checklist below to identify how you want to use your social media accounts:

○ Build and engage my community

　　○ Connect and converse with friends and family

　　○ Connect and converse with a broader community

　　○ Follow and connect with prominent community members

　　○ Share articles and posts by community members who inspire you

　　○ Invite community members to in-person events

　　○ Build or participate in a movement of people with my identity or interests

- Promote the work of other creatives, especially those just starting out!

- Grow the audience for my work

  - Increase traffic to my website or blog

  - Increase sign ups for my newsletter or subscriptions to my podcast, etc.

  - Build my reputation as a trusted expert in my field

- Better understand my industry

  - Keep current with relevant industry news

  - Learn best practices from established creators

  - Gather and share resources

- Share my creative process and finished work

  - Create a visual experience / feeling for my followers to give them a sense of my creative identity

  - Highlight works in progress

  - Offer insight into my creative process and inspiration

  - Release or debut new work like blog posts, songs, videos, or podcast episodes

- Sell products or services

- Promote events, sales, and gatherings

Create a plan for each platform

Once you've decided which platforms you want to join and use for your project, create a plan for each. This will help keep you focused and ensure that each platform represents your overall brand and project vision, mission, voice, and values.

Platform #1

Platform name:

Primary type of content: *Ex. Images, text, video*

Goals for your presence on this platform:

1.

2.

3.

Reflect: My goals for this platform relate to my overall mission, vision, and values by . . .

People will be interested to follow me because . . .

I will build community on this platform by . . .

When people look at my feed I want them to feel . . .

List 3 to 5 different types of content you will share on this platform

Ex. *New blog posts, articles that inspire me, behind the scenes work, works in progress*

Platform #2

Platform name:

Primary type of content: *Ex. Images, text, video*

Goals for your presence on this platform:

1.

2.

3.

Reflect: My goals for this platform relate to my overall mission, vision, and values by . . .

People will be interested to follow me because . . .

I will build community on this platform by . . .

When people look at my feed I want them to feel . . .

List 3 to 5 different types of content you will share on this platform

Ex. *New blog posts, articles that inspire me, behind the scenes work, works in progress*

Platform #3

Platform name:

Primary type of content: *Ex. Images, text, video*

Goals for your presence on this platform:

1.

2.

3.

Reflect: My goals for this platform relate to my overall mission, vision, and values by . . .

People will be interested to follow me because . . .

I will build community on this platform by . . .

When people look at my feed I want them to feel . . .

List 3 to 5 different types of content you will share on this platform

Ex. *New blog posts, articles that inspire me, behind the scenes work, works in progress*

Social media account set up

These are the assets you will need to set up your profile:

- ◯ Header image for profile page

- ◯ Profile photo

- ◯ Bio

- ◯ Link to website

- ◯ Logo or visual brand

- ◯ Contact information

Brainstorm posts

Depending on your goals for your social media presence, you may choose to brainstorm more specific posts for certain events, sales, or updates as they arise. Use the exercises below to generate ideas for posts:

Who are you as a creative? Write 3 short posts (1-2 sentences) that can enable your followers to get to know you:

1.

2.

3.

What are images that could go with these posts?

What/who inspires you? Write 3 short posts highlighting sources of your inspiration:

1.

2.

3.

What are images that could go with these posts?

What's important to you as a creative? Write 3 short posts that illustrate your values:

1.

2.

3.

What are images that could go with these posts?

What are you working on right now? Write 3 short posts that illustrate your process/work in progress:

1.

2.

3.

What are images that could go with these posts?

What could be helpful to others in your community? Write 3 short posts sharing information, articles, or facts that have been helpful to you and may be helpful to others:

1.

2.

3.

What are images that could go with these posts?

Build excitement for your project

You can create multiple posts to build excitement for a new piece of content or product, such as a video for your band, a new podcast episode, or a new product in your shop. Think about an aspect of your project you want to promote and write a series of posts promoting it—think broadly and boldly when brainstorming your posts. Not all of these posts may be a fit for every project, but use these prompts to get your ideas down on paper.

What I am promoting:

Teaser post: Pique your audiences' interest without telling them exactly what it is

Post:

Image:

Announcement post: The big reveal! What is it, why is it cool, when will it be available

Post:

Image:

Behind the scenes: Give insight into the making of or inspiration for your project

Post:

Image:

Reminder post: Remind your audience about the launch of the new project/item and keep the excitement building

Post:

Image:

Launch post: It's here! Hurrah! Here's how to get it!

Post:

Image:

Call to Action post: Help me / join me to do XYZ activities!

Post:

Image:

Community response post: Highlight how someone in your community is using/ enjoying what you made or great feedback you received

Post:

Image:

Thank you post: Express gratitude to your community for their support of your project

Post:

Image:

Follow up post: Missed the big launch? There's still time to enjoy and be a part of the excitement!

Post:

Image:

Stay engaged: Want to be more involved in this project? Here's how—could be a related project, story, or an invitation to an event

Post:

Image:

Social media calendar

To keep yourself organized, use a calendar to plan out your social media posts for a week, or even a month, so you can build up a consistent voice and presence on each platform. You can post the same content across each platform, but since each has their own format and some have character or time limits, a calendar can also help you craft slightly different messaging for each.

Many platforms, or social media management software, enable you to schedule posts in advance. This means you can ensure you are posting consistently, even when your schedule is busy.

Separate from your calendar, you may want to create a spreadsheet with ideas for posts, links, images, quotes, and anything else that inspires and relates to your social media goals so you always have something ready to share.

You can also copy the sample social media calendar in the spreadsheet at http://microcosm.pub/qydj to use for your own needs

Building community on social media

Online communities are similar to real-life communities in that they take time to cultivate and build. To build your online community:

- Join and participate in groups related to your field or project

- Follow hashtags that are related to your project

- Find and follow your peers and people you respect

- Comment on peoples' posts and answer their questions when they ask

- If someone in your community makes something new, post about it, share the link, and tag them

- Be genuine and polite in your interactions

Social Media Calendar

Day	Date	Time	Platform	Text	Link	Character Count	Image
Monday							
Tuesday							
Wednesday							
Thursday							
Friday							
Saturday							
Sunday							

Inviting others to share your project:

- Once you have built a solid relationship with members of your network, you can ask them to share your project, especially if you have something new coming out

- Message members of your network directly and politely ask them if they would be willing to share

- Tell them how your project relates to their interests and what they share on their feed

- Provide them with a sample post—copying and pasting makes it much easier to share. The post should include:

  - A short project description that builds excitement about your project

  - The link to your project

  - Images

- Thank them for their consideration whether they agree or not

Social media milestones checklist

Not all of these accomplishments might apply to your project, but use this checklist to acknowledge and celebrate your little wins!

◯ Upload your photo and/or logo to your accounts

◯ Research relevant hashtags for your project

◯ Post using a relevant hashtag

◯ Follow a relevant hashtag

◯ Get "verified" on Facebook

◯ Get a vanity URL for a Facebook or Youtube account

◯ Get mentioned in someone's Instagram story

◯ Get retweeted on Twitter

- ◯ Meet with a person in your field who you don't know in "real" life
- ◯ Engage in a meaningful conversation with a follower or someone you follow
- ◯ Have a post shared by someone you respect in your field
- ◯ Have over 100 followers (who are actual people, not bots)
- ◯ Receive a newsletter sign up from a social media post
- ◯ Make a sale from a social media post

A note about "influencers" and social media "celebrities"

Some social media users with a large following choose to monetize it by receiving free products and being paid to promote them through a mention. While these posts more frequently have to be disclosed as the paid advertisements that they are, the lines between paid promotion and authentic endorsement on social media can be murky. Often influencers have agents that represent them and will charge a significant amount of money for advertising.

Exercise caution when thinking about if, how, and when to engage influencers and paid advertising in general—they won't necessarily grow your community or sell your products and may not be entirely in-line with your brand or values.

Chapter Three Checklist

- ◯ Create a marketing campaign creative brief, which gives you an overview of your marketing efforts and strategies
- ◯ Create a pitch that describes you and the unique characteristics of your project. This is your chance to tell your story
- ◯ Build your digital presence
  - ◯ Set up and utilize social media accounts
  - ◯ Build and launch your website
  - ◯ Create an email newsletter

PRESS OUTREACH
ENGAGING TRADITIONAL MEDIA

E ngaging traditional media, whether in print or online, is another way to reach a wider audience for your project. Building press contacts is about building relationships with journalists and editors. It is up to you to demonstrate to them how your project matches the needs of their publication, site, or program.

Define Your Goals for Press Coverage

Start with defining your goals for press coverage. Some examples may include:

- Reviews for a new album, publication, or event

- Publicity in advance of an event

- Appearing as an "expert guest" on programs, podcasts, or blogs

- Reaching a specific community served by niche publications

Write 2 -3 goals for press coverage here:

1.

2.

3.

Identify Publications that Are a Fit for Your Project

Once you are clear on your goals, identify publications, blogs, podcasts, radio shows, and television programs that cover projects and events similar to yours. Musician Greta Gertler, explains how she identifies and prioritizes publications to reach out to, "I follow artists that are getting press and who are similar to the ones I am promoting. I see where they are getting written up and target that press."

Marisha Chinsky, a musician and PR agent, recommends getting advice from friends and colleagues who have gone through a similar process to you. "Hold an informal focus group with community members who are familiar with or passionate about the realm of your project. If you're starting an art gallery, tap into your artist contacts to ask where they go for art news. If you're opening a yoga studio, ask another local yoga studio and their patrons if they have sources of information in the media. Advice is free, people are keen to help, and communities are supportive if you're friendly and respectful of people's time and opinions."

Look at who writes and edits the sections you are interested in and then look at the publication's masthead, as well as journalists' and editors' social media accounts, for their contact information. There are also many groups for freelance writers that share contact information for major publications.

Make a list of relevant publications and editors to pitch to. You may want to format this into a spreadsheet so you can easily sort, search, and track feedback from pitches.

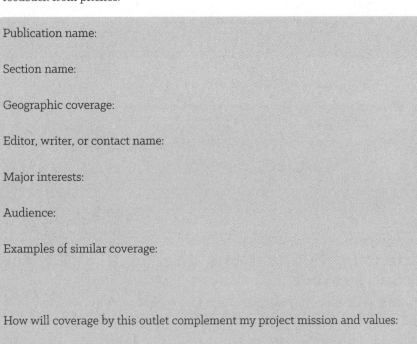

Publication name:

Section name:

Geographic coverage:

Editor, writer, or contact name:

Major interests:

Audience:

Examples of similar coverage:

How will coverage by this outlet complement my project mission and values:

Craft Your Pitch

Before you start reaching out to the publications that you have identified as a good fit, you need to craft your pitch. Your pitch summarizes the story you want to tell about your project, provides basic information, and lets an editor know why it would be a good fit for their publication.

Marisha Chinsky shared advice about how to craft your pitch to editors, "Press releases are less relevant than in the past. With social media, plus the 24/7 news cycle that reporters must keep up with, a concise, punchy pitch email is more effective than a wordy press release."

She advises to tailor your pitch: "It's worthwhile to connect your pitch to a news hook like a new product launch, store opening, a milestone like your 1,000th customer, or something about your product or service that's connected to a holiday and public event. Maybe you're selling your artisanal soda at the local county fair? Or offering discounts on Halloween?"

Often stories that have specific, local interest are easier to pitch, especially to hyper-local newsletters, papers, and blogs. When you are pitching, don't discount the power of images. High-quality images will often sell your story for you.

To prepare to create your pitch, make notes of the following information:

Name of project:

Person to contact about it (most likely you):

Release date for your project or product:

Location and time (if an event):

One-sentence description of your project:

Why is this interesting or relevant for this editor/publication and their readers:

Press pitch template

Use the following template to structure your pitch

Subject line: [Pitch: Catchy headline no more than 65 characters]

Dear [Editor Name],

Paragraph 1:

- Fact, statistic, quote, or statement to introduce your project and grab their attention

- 1 - 2 sentence project description and relevant information

- Why it is important, timely, and relevant to their interests and publication

Paragraph 2:

- 1 - 2 sentences about you and why you are cool and unique and the publication should care not only about your project, but about you

- Social proof - community response, other publications that have covered your project

- Thank them for their consideration

After salutation:

- Contact information

- Relevant links

Overall, keep your communication polite and brief. If you haven't heard from someone after a week, follow up once and then move on.

As you start to reach out, prioritize your press outreach list. Start with local or niche outlets that are more likely to give you coverage. Pitching to smaller, friendlier outlets will help you build confidence and relationships and give you a better understanding of what editors and journalists need from you.

Keep in touch with journalists and editors and keep track of where they work. The media world is small and people move around a lot and work for a variety of publications. Keep your spreadsheet up to date so that you don't lose a good contact!

Press Outreach Tools Checklist

- ( ) Calendar for deadlines, submissions, and pitches
- ( ) High-resolution, high-quality photos for print and web publication
  - ( ) In an email - link these images instead of attach them - editors will often delete emails with large attachments from people they don't know
- ( ) Press resource on your website
  - ( ) Downloadable photos
  - ( ) Quotes
  - ( ) Fact sheet about your project
- ( ) Examples of past press coverage

Chapter Four Checklist

- ( ) Brainstorm your goals for engaging with traditional media forms
- ( ) Research and identify journalists and publications that complement your mission and values
- ( ) Develop a new pitch specific for this purpose, that outlines you, your project, and where you are headed
- ( ) Keep track of who you contact and when so you know when to follow-up and who is excited about your work

TELL THE STORY OF YOUR PROJECT IN NUMBERS

GET COMFORTABLE WITH THE FINANCIAL SIDE OF YOUR PROJECT

Understanding and planning for the financial aspects of your project supports your mission, vision, and values. Even if your project is a non-profit project or you identify as an anti-capitalist, you still need resources to make your project happen. The clearer you get about money and finances, the easier it is to feel in control of your project and make decisions that are in line with your values.

Assess Your Feelings About Money

The first step in creating a financial plan for your project is to understand your own relationship to money. Is there a part of you that wants to run away screaming as soon as you hear the words "financial," "money" or "finance?" Or, are you a careful budgeter who already tracks your personal expenses?

It can be scary to look yourself (and your bank account) straight in the eye and acknowledge your weaknesses, but you might also find that you have stronger financial skills than you thought. When you know where you need to grow, and where you are strong financially, you can take a proactive stance to tackling your project's budget and finances.

Before diving in to creating a budget for your project, setting prices for the product you produce, hiring people to work with you, paying yourself, and fundraising, take a few minutes, or hours, to reflect on these questions:

Think about your current financial plan:

Do you have a personal or project budget?

Do you follow it? Why or why not?

How diligent are you in tracking your day-to-day expenses?

How does the word "budget" make you feel? Where do those feelings come from?

Think about your financial history:

What are your proudest achievements?

What are big financial lessons you learned the hard way?

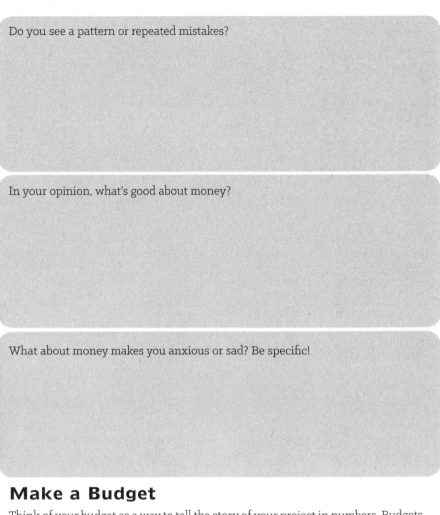

Do you see a pattern or repeated mistakes?

In your opinion, what's good about money?

What about money makes you anxious or sad? Be specific!

Make a Budget

Think of your budget as a way to tell the story of your project in numbers. Budgets capture what you have and what you need to make a project happen, and, as you track your expenses and income, the growth and progress of your project.

Note: Remember that as you begin to generate income, you may need to begin to pay taxes, which qualifies as an expense. While you may not be sure of the actual amount at first, add it as a line item on your budget to fill in when you have a sense of your flow of income and expenses.

Budget brainstorm

Make a list of everything you need to buy or the services you need to procure to accomplish with your project:

Do you need a particular type of material or equipment? To rent space? To hire someone with a specialized skill? To pay for postage or travel? Don't forget that you will also need to pay yourself!

Organize your list into as many broad categories as you need. Group similar expenses together.

For example, paint, brushes, ladders and drop cloths for your mural painting project could all go under "Supplies," whereas the website, posters and invitations that you will send to promote the mural's opening could be grouped together under "Publicity."

Category 1:

Category 2:

Category 3:

Generating income

What is income? Income is all resources that you gather to support your project. Your budget is a work of fiction until you start to bring in money and support for your project. Tackling the question of income is important because it helps you focus on exactly how much money, or support, you need to find to make the project happen.

At the beginning of the income planning process you may not know the answer to all of these questions, and your income streams can expand as the project develops. Later in this section we will cover the major categories of income: in-kind support, bartering, earning income through selling your work and charging for your time, and raising contributed income through fundraising.

List all the sources of income you expect to bring in here:

Clarify Your Income Strategy
Write 1-2 sentences in response to each of these questions.

How do you expect your project to make money or support itself?

What parts of the project will you complete yourself?

Will you trade goods and services with others, for which parts of the project?

Do you need to ask for volunteers to help with a particular part of the project? Such as theatre users or to help promote the project.

Can you set aside a percentage of your income each month to help support your project? How much will you contribute per month and how will you adjust your lifestyle and spending habits to accommodate this?

Do you plan to fundraise to cover your project expenses—what are some sources of funding that you might be able to access?

From the list above, organize income into earned, contributed aka donations, and in-kind support if applicable.

Earned

Source 1:

Source 2:

Source 3:

Contributed

Source 1:

Source 2:

Source 3:

In-kind Support

Service or Item 1:

Service or Item 2:

Service or Item 3:

Set up a budget in a spreadsheet

Once you have your expenses organized into categories, format your budget in a spreadsheet program, like Microsoft Excel, Google Sheets, etc. Spreadsheets are important, even for simple project budgets. They can easily perform important functions like adding up multiple columns of numbers and calculating percentages. Take a few hours to learn the basics of using spreadsheets—there are many free online tutorials available to help you. Use formulas to save you from entering the same information over and over.

Below is a basic project budget template that you can put into Excel or the spreadsheet program of your choice. Input the lists and categories from your brainstorm. Add categories and items as you need. You can find a template online at http://microcosm.pub/qydj to copy and use yourself.

Expenses

Category 1:

Item	Price	Quantity	Totals

Category 1 Subtotal:

Category 2:

Item	Price	Quantity	Totals

Category 2 Subtotal:

Category 3:

Item	Price	Quantity	Totals

Category 3 Subtotal:

Expense Total:

Income

Category 1:

Item	Price	Quantity	Totals

Category 1 Subtotal:

Category 2:

Item	Price	Quantity	Totals

Category 2 Subtotal :

Category 3:

Item	Price	Quantity	Totals

Category 3 Subtotal :

Income Total :

Profit / Loss (Income Minus Expenses) :

Spending Record

A budget is an outline of your project. As you start to spend money and time on your project, save your receipts and track your expenses so you have a clear idea of how much you are spending and on what. This will also help you at tax time, when you can show how much you put into your business if you want to write it off!

There are many free budgeting and expense tracker apps available for your phone or computer that link to your bank accounts and enable you to automatically upload and categorize receipts, which can make your life a lot easier.

While it can be tempting to put off cataloguing expenses until the end of a project, try to record them in real time (apps make this very easy) or set aside an hour a week to take care of your financial reporting. This will save you time and angst in the long run.

On the next page, you'll find an example expense tracking worksheet that you can easily put into a spreadsheet program. Many apps will automatically generate a spreadsheet from your uploaded expenses as well.

Plan to Barter Better

Bartering is a powerful way to build support and goodwill for your project and is a specific type of transactional relationship that is mutually beneficial to both parties. Use this worksheet to plan what you need from a barter and what you will offer in return. Use these terms to form the basis of a written agreement with the person you identify to trade with.

Make barter/trade plan:

Specific skills/resources I need for my project:

People I know or could reach out to who offer these skills/resources:

Working with this person will benefit my project because:

Expense tracking worksheet

Merchant/ Vendor Name	Expense Description	Expense Date	Expense Type	Expense Amount	Receipt or Invoice

If I were to pay for this skill/resource, it would be valued at: $____

Skills/resources I can offer in return:

If someone paid me for this skill resource, it would be valued at: $____

If this person works with me, their project will benefit because:

Date by when barter will be finished:

Earned Income: Pricing Your Work

Earned income is what we most often think of as "making money." It is money you receive from selling a product or a service. For example, a band generates earned income when they sell tickets, CDs and t-shirts. To ensure you generate the income you need for your project, plan carefully about how much to charge for that product. You need to have an idea of how much your product costs to make, the size of your audience, how much they are willing to pay for the product you are offering to them, and how often they will want it. When you have knowledge of price and audience, you can avoid overestimating the amount of money you will make from sales and under-pricing your work.

Use the knowledge you already have about your project to estimate your audience and set your prices. For example, if your band usually draws 40 people and shows in your area usually cost $5 it would be reasonable to expect that you could bring in $200 from that show. Does $200 cover your expenses? Is your band popular enough that you could charge more? Or are you just starting out and think you may need to charge less to draw a larger audience? Look at the prices of other projects like your own. How much are people willing to pay? How popular is a particular item?

Antonio Ramos from Brooklyn Soda Works laid out basic factors to consider when pricing your work, "What does it cost to make? How long does it take to make it? What profit can you make from your product at a price people will pay without compromising the essential nature of your project?"As you think about prices remember these two important pieces advice from other DIY business owners:

- Beware of extremes in pricing: Do not offer so many discounts you can't stay in business, but understand that if you price your product too high, you may exclude customers and many may be reluctant to buy it

- Protect yourself and your time: Require customers to pre-pay

Product pricing guidelines worksheet

Use this worksheet to help understand how much it costs to make your product and better determine your prices.

How much do the raw materials to make your item cost?

How much time does it take to make your item?

If you were to assign yourself an hourly rate for making the item, how much would it be? *See pricing your time and services exercise later in this chapter*

What are the overhead costs that impact the price of this object, such as studio space rent or equipment rental? (For example, if you need to rent a studio for two hours to make your item, that rental cost should factor into the price)

What is the standard price for a product like yours in your field?

How much are your customers willing to pay?

How low of a price would make your customers decide your item is not worth their time?

Product pricing formula

Using your answers to the questions above, use this formula to help determine a price for your product, and then adjust. The standard retail markup for an item is 50%.

_____ +
Cost of materials needed to make your item

_____ +
Hourly rate for the time it takes to make it

_____ +
Overhead costs

_____ = your starting price
50% standard retail markup

Once you come up with this price, compare it to the price of similar products. Reflect on these questions:

- If your price is higher, is your product higher quality, use special materials, or a special skill?

- If your price is equivalent to that of other products, do you feel that is fair?

- If your price is lower, do you feel this will help make your product more attractive or will it cheapen what you offer?

You can experiment with "charm pricing," which is ending the price with a 9 or a 5, for example, $35.99, as it has been shown to entice buyers.

A note on pricing: Unfortunately, because creatives are often not taught to value themselves or their work, you might find many products similar to yours are priced absurdly low. Resist the urge to underprice your product to compete, this will only prevent your project from becoming sustainable long-term and frustrate you—instead focus on how you can demonstrate the unique value of what you make.

You can also refer to pricing guides if you work in a specific discipline, such as crafts, visual arts, or music. The conventional wisdom about pricing can vary depending on the discipline, but remember "conventional wisdom" doesn't necessarily cover your circumstance or the unique value you bring to your work. People are not necessarily rational when it comes to money, so you may need to adjust your prices as you learn what works for your market and community.

Pricing terminology

In order be better able to discuss prices with buyers, suppliers and retailers and to build your confidence in the prices you set it is helpful to be familiar with the following terms and ideas about pricing:

Total cost to produce your item: this is the basic cost of materials, labor and time it takes for you to make 78704em. This should not be your price, but you should know how much each item takes to produce, which is also called "cost of goods."

Wholesale price: This is the price at which you offer your product to retailers. You will be offering your items to retailers at a "markup" price on your base cost. The markup should cover your overhead, such as your studio space and your tools. There's no hard and fast formula for determining the wholesale price, but it can range from 100 to 300 percent of the total cost, depending on the product you are offering.

Retail price: This is the price you suggest to retailers to sell your item. This can be twice or even three times the wholesale price. Remember, retailers take a percentage of the sale of your item to cover their costs. In addition, when you are selling your item yourself, such as through a website or in person, you should offer it at the retail price. You don't want to undersell yourself or the retailers that are carrying your work!

Research pricing strategies for your specific field and discuss with others making similar work to your own about how they set their prices. The most important aspect of setting your prices is to cover your costs and to feel good about the prices you set.

Earned Income: Paying Yourself

Paying yourself fairly for your work is an important step in building a sustainable, creative life. When you pay yourself you recognize the time and effort that goes into your work and acknowledge that your skills and expertise have value. In addition, your project can be based on offering up your time, talents, or a particular service, such as writing grant proposals, event planning, designing a website or composing songs. Build confidence in yourself so that you can be compensated fairly.

Pricing your time and services

There are no hard and fast formulas for determining how much to charge hourly or for project-based prices. However, there are strategies you can use to get an estimate and refine your prices from there.

A simple strategy for pricing your time is based on overhead costs and amount of time you want to work.

To get a sense of your value, reflect on the following questions:

Clarify what you are selling. What is the exact service you are offering?

Consider your experience and expertise. Do you have a perspective or level of experience that is not common for your field?

How does what you're offering bring value to your customer's lives? How does it help them achieve their goals?

Next, use this worksheet to help understand how much to charge for your services in order to determine your prices:

List your overhead costs such as tools, software, studio rent, insurance:

List your living expenses for the year, month and week:

Determine how many hours a week you want to work:

Divide to get your starting number for your hourly rate

For example:

Total Monthly Expenses: $2,000

Hours a Week: 30

Weeks in a Month: 4
$2,000 ÷ 4 = $500

$500 ÷ 30 = $17 basic hourly rate to cover expenses

However, you cannot bill your clients for every hour you spend working—they don't pay for you checking your email, networking, learning new skills, and everything else you do that is related to your project, but not the specific job they hired you to do. Thus your "billable" time should cover your expenses incurred during "non-billable" hours. Therefore, I may determine that I will work about 15 hours a week on my clients' specific projects, so I could raise my rate to $30 an hour to cover those expenses, so my calculations would look like this:

Monthly Expenses: $2,000

Billable Hours a Week: 15

Weeks in a Month: 4

$2,000 ÷ 4 = $500
$500 ÷ 15 = $33 hourly rate to cover expenses for billable and non-billable time

Once you have an idea of how much you need to charge to cover your expenses, find out the going rate for your field. Talk to other professionals in your field about how they determine their prices. This is especially important if you are just starting out. You can also reach out to clients that you know and trust or people you know how they hire creative professionals who do a kind of work similar to yours. Search on the internet using general search terms and using websites where freelancers advertise their services or companies post ads for freelancers to give you a sense.

Service pricing terminology
There are several terms to know related to pricing your services that will enable you to discuss prices easily with those who are hiring you. Pricing your services can be done on a time basis, a project basis, or a package basis.

Time-based is how much you charge per hour for your services. When you have an idea of your hourly rate, you can determine the basis for what to charge for a specific project. Hourly rates are good for projects that take a fixed amount of time to accomplish, such as administrative support, installing an art piece, or outreach.

Project-based is a price based for an entire project that has a concrete end point, such as designing a brochure. When pricing based on a project you want to calculate about how many hours it will take, as well as your overhead such as the tools and space you use to create it.

Package-based is similar to project-based pricing, but it puts more conditions around a project, especially in case the person who is hiring you asks for more consultations, revisions or questions than you originally bargained for. You offer a certain amount of time or number of consultations for a flat-fee and, if your client demands more changes or wants additional services, you can charge by the hour or an agreed-upon additional fee.

The key to pricing your services is to trust that your time is valuable and to communicate that value to others. You have skills, creativity, and expertise to offer to your potential clients. If you are part of a community that is based on a barter economy be sure you explain clearly the time that it takes for you to make your product and the expertise you bring to the service that you are offering to ensure you get a fair trade. Be upfront about your needs. As a creative person educate yourself and your community members about your worth. You must value yourself first before expecting anyone else to.

Chapter Five Checklist

◯ Take time to assess, and possibly unlearn, the cultural condition you have surrounding money. This will help you get comfortable with the financial needs of your project, help you advocate for your own financial needs, and assess the financial viability of your project

◯ Make a budget to carefully track income and expenditures, whether that money is coming from donations, crowd-sourcing, product sales, tools and supplies, bartering, etc.

◯ Learn how to value to your work and time dedicated to your project

  ◯ Developing pricing standards

  ◯ Developing an hourly rate and a strategy to pay yourself

FUNDRAISING

ontributed income, or donations, is another way to raise money for your project. However, donations are not free money! They still require some kind of exchange and engagement. For example, if you are applying for public funding, like grants, the project will most often need to have some kind of public benefit. If you are planning a campaign for crowdfunding or ongoing support, you will want to produce a product, service, or reward that your supporters get in exchange for giving.

Fundraising Campaign Planning

Before completing the next exercises on planning a crowdfunding campaign and applying for grants, answer the questions below to understand your motivations and needs for raising money:

How Much?

How much money do you need to raise to cover your project expenses?

What will the money specifically pay for?

How much money do you have to invest in fundraising (for example, to put into producing rewards, hiring writing help, etc.)?

When?

What phase of the project are you fundraising for?

When do you expect the project to be completed?

How much time do you have to invest in fundraising?

Who?

Who are the people most likely to support this project?

Why?

What makes this project compelling and what would motivate your extended network and community to support it?

Crowdfunding

"Crowdfunding" is a strategy to raise money from your network to support your project. There are many different crowdfunding platforms that have different funding models available. The two major types are either a **campaign model** or a **subscription model**.

A **crowdfunding campaign** is a time-based campaign that raises money towards a set goal to support a specific initiative or part of your project, such as publishing a book or releasing an album.

A **subscription or membership** collects regularly scheduled contributions from your network, most often monthly, to support your on-going or serial work, such as a webcomic or podcast, and enables you to have regular income from your project.

Before starting either kind of campaign, reflect on the following questions:

Am I launching a new project or looking for on-going support for a current project?

Do I need a specific amount of money to launch a project or on-going support to keep my project sustainable?

What are my goals for launching a crowdfunding initiative at this time?

If you are looking to launch a project, a time-bound, crowdfunding campaign may be a better fit for you. If you already have an established project and are looking to make it sustainable and connect more regularly with your supporters, a membership-style initiative might make more sense for you.

Plan a Crowdfunding Campaign

To plan a short-term crowdfunding campaign, follow these steps.

Step 1: Make your budget

How much money do you need to raise to make this project successful? (Be honest!)

What will you use the money for?

Step 2: Assess your network

Make a list of the different groups of people in your life: family, school, work, different interests and hobbies:

Make a list of specific people in each of those groups.

How many people are there?

How many friends do you have on social media networks?

Based on the size of your network, how much money do you think you can raise?

Step 3: Determine your goal and your giving levels
Base your goal on your project budget and the amount of money you think you can raise from your network.

The total you need to raise is:

About how many people are in your extended network?

• Determine the different levels of giving you will need to meet your goal. How many people can you realistically expect to give at each level?

• Break your reward levels and the number of people you expect to give at each level into a giving pyramid like the example below.

• Customize the number of levels, participants, and giving amount to suit each specific part of the project.

Giving pyramid based on a $5,500 goal and participation from 135 people

2 people - $500

3 people - $250

10 people - $100

20 people - $50

50 people - $25

50 people - $10

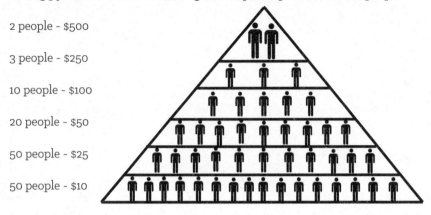

Step 4: Describe and pitch your project

Refer back to the marketing and branding exercises for help with these questions.

Answer this question in one catchy, compelling sentence: What is my project and why is it worthy of attention and support?

This will be your tagline for your project.

Expand that sentence into 1 to 2 short paragraphs in which you answer these questions:

- What is my project and why is it worthy of attention and support?

- What impact will this project have on the world?

- Why am I uniquely qualified to accomplish this project?

- Why is this project important now?

This will be your project description.

Base the script for your pitch video on the description and the elements below:

Make a 2-to-3 minute pitch video that includes these elements:

- A personal introduction

- A succinct introduction to the project and its goals and timeline

- The impact and importance of the project

- Show or describe the rewards

- Ask directly for support

Step 5: Determine your rewards

Rewards should be related to your project and help you pre-sell and promote it, as well as give your contributors a good feeling about it.

Determine your rewards for each level of contribution. Factor in the price of creating and shipping the reward using this equation:

Contribution level—production of the reward—shipping = what you earn for your project

Organize your rewards into a table like the example below to compare and keep track

$10 Level	$25 Level	$50 Level	$100 Level	$250 Level	$500 Level
Reward #1	Reward #1	Reward #1	Reward #1	Reward #1	Reward #1
	Reward #2	Reward #2	Reward #2	Reward #2	Reward #2
		Reward #3	Reward #3	Reward #3	Reward #3
			Reward #4	Reward #4	Reward #4
				Reward #5	Reward #5
					Reward #6

For each reward level give it a project related title and write a catchy, one-sentence description.

Reward level and title:

Description:

Step 6: Set up your campaign site and spread the word
Split your campaign into 4 phases:

- Quiet phase (*first 1 to 2 weeks of the launch*)

- Public phase (*middle of campaign*)

- Final push (*Last 7 to 10 days of campaign*)

- Follow up (*after the campaign*)

Quiet Phase
Make a list of your closest community, friends, supporters and fans.

Draft an email or a script for a phone call to tell these close supporters about the campaign and invite them to get involved early.

Include:

- Warm introduction

- Brief description of the campaign and project

- Direct ask for support

- Why you are inviting them to get involved

- What their support means to you

- How their early support will help you achieve your goal

- Thank you

Public Phase

Send an email to your email list announcing the campaign

Include:

- Warm introduction

- Brief description of the campaign and project

- Excitement about the momentum the campaign has gained so far

- Direct ask for support and sharing the campaign

- Why you are inviting them to get involved

- What their support means to you

- Thank you

Preplan blog entries, email newsletters, and social media posts to engage your network with the campaign.

Final Push

Follow up with people who you invited to give and have not yet

Reminder to email list:

- Thank them for their support so far

- Remind them of the deadline

- Encourage them to share

For the last 7-to-10 days of the campaign, make a list of 7-to-10 reasons to give to your project and push one reason out a day until the end of the campaign

1.

2.

3.

4.

5.

6.

7.

8.

9.

10.

Follow Up

- After your campaign ends, post "thank you for your support" posts on social media

- Send a thank you email to your supporters and let them know when they can expect their rewards

- Add supporters to your mailing list

- Invite them to project-related events and keep them up-to-date with project-related news

Building Ongoing Support: Setting Up a Membership or Subscription Program

This kind of on-going support is also referred to as a "drip campaign" because ongoing support "drips" in and builds up overtime. This type of fundraising may be best suited to projects or artists who already have a network who create and release work on a regular or serial basis, such as a podcast, web video series, zine, or comic. You may consider launching a membership program following a crowdfunding campaign so that you can cultivate ongoing support and connection to your network.

Step 1: Determine your motivation, goals, and budget

To help articulate what you want to achieve and your motivation for setting up a membership program, answer the following questions:

How does your work lend itself to a membership program?

What will you share on this platform that would be different (and more exclusive) than social media or your website?

How will you benefit as a creative person from a membership program?

How will your community benefit from being able to support and connect with you as a creator through this platform?

List three goals for launching a membership program

They could include making a certain amount of income a month, adding a certain number of supporters per month, connecting more personally with your community, or creating a place to get feedback on work in progress. Remember to keep your goals SMART

1.

2.

3.

Set a monthly fundraising goal:
It's okay to start realistic—you can increase your goal as your network grows

Step 2: Assess your network
Make a list of all the different groups of people in your life who support your project.

For example, coworkers, podcast listeners, social media followers.

1.

2.

3.

4.

5.

Next, list what would motivate each group to support your membership campaign:

1.

2.

3.

4.

5.

Step 3: Define your membership experience and set your membership levels

Define 3 - 5 tiers for membership support and list the benefits and exclusive content each will receive:

Tier 1:
Ex. $5/month

Tier 2:

Ex. $10/month

Tier 3:

Ex. $20/month

When determining these levels take into account the time, money, and other resources needed to create and deliver your rewards.

Step 4: Describe and pitch your project

Refer back to the marketing and branding exercises for help with these questions.

Answer this question in one catchy, compelling sentence: What is my project and why is it worthy of attention and support?

This will be your tagline for your project.

Expand that sentence into 1 to 2 short paragraphs in which you answer these questions:

- What is my project/work and why is it worthy of attention and support?

- How will I use this platform to connect and share with my community and fans on a regular basis?

- Why am I uniquely qualified to accomplish this project?

- Why is this project/work important now?

This will be your project description.

Base the script for your pitch video on the description and the elements below:

Make a 2 to 3 minute pitch video that includes these elements:

- A personal introduction to you as a creative person

- A succinct introduction to the work you make and what you'll be sharing on the platform

- Why you are excited to connect with your community in this way

- Show or describe the membership levels

- Describe how your community's support will enable you to grow your creative practice

Step 5: Launch and spread the word

Let your network know about the opportunity to get involved with your work, how excited you are to connect with them through a membership platform, and how you have the chance to grow as a creator with their support.

Create your outreach using the prompts below:

Send an email to your email list announcing the campaign

Include:

- Warm introduction

- Brief description your creative project

- Excitement about the opportunity to join as a member/ongoing supporter

- How this support will help you grow as a creator

- What they will receive for their support

- Direct ask for support

- Thank you

Write 3 social media posts announcing your membership opportunity. Each one could speak to a different goal or a different benefit for joining:

Post 1:

Image to go with post:

Post 2:

Image to go with post:

Post 3:

Image to go with post:

Step 6: Nurture your network and members

Keeping your membership base engaged and building a relationship with them will help you build and keep ongoing support. Continuously creating content can be stressful, so to make it easier, plan what you will share in advance.

Use the calendar template on page 133 to organize and plan what you will offer your members each month:

Think beyond your project! Your members have decided to support you on an ongoing basis because they want to connect with you as a creative person.

Writing a Grant Proposal

Grants are awards that are given by public entities and philanthropic foundations to advance their mission and provide some kind of public benefit. Funders tend to give out money that advances their mission, and are more likely to allocate funds to your project if you have demonstrated some level of success, either in this project or another project. Every grant proposal is different because every fund has a different mission, guidelines, and endowments. Venturing into the world of grants can seem daunting, but once you get used to it, it will become more straightforward.

Calendar Template

	Week 1	Week 2	Week 3	Week 4
Public Content				
Tier 1				
Tier 2				
Tier 3				

To create a strong grant application, keep the following in mind:

- Read eligibility requirements and grant application instructions carefully

- Follow all the instructions, right down to picky formatting details

- Use clear, succinct language in your application

- Think about why and how your project supports the funder's mission

- If you have questions about the application process, reach out to the program officer or grant administrator

- Be courteous in all of your interactions—being difficult or entitled will not help you get funding

The exercises below will equip you with basic proposal language that you can customize for each specific application.

Brainstorm 3-to-5 ideas to engage your members outside of the regular content you are creating and sharing

A special "how to" lesson or webinar? Meetup? Special greeting cards?

1.

2.

3.

4.

5.

Executive summary

This is the most important part of your proposal. It provides a summary of the entire application and all the key information in a single paragraph. In addition, it needs to hook the reader and "sell" them on your idea.

To construct your summary:

Write one to two sentences that summarize the problem or issue your project addresses:

Write one to two sentences that describe how your project offers a solution to that problem or explores those issues in an innovative fashion:

Write one to two sentences to make your funding request—how much money you are asking for and what you will do with it:

Write one to two sentences to discuss your expertise, experience and qualifications that will enable you to complete this project:

Project narrative

The narrative builds on your summary and gives the reader more information about what you plan to do. It provides the basic who, what, when, why and how of your project and makes the case for support.

Build your narrative:

The project's mission, goal(s), objectives and history make up the "what" of the project.

Break each down for added clarity.

State the mission of your project:

Refer to the earlier section on crafting your mission statement

State your goal for the project:

The goal is the big idea that your project grapples with

Write three objectives that support that goal. Objectives are measurable outcomes that are specific and achievable within a certain time frame:

1.

2.

3.

Project history

Write a paragraph describing the project's history. Reference your mission, vision, and values statements for guidance.

To help craft your paragraph answer to the following questions:

When did you start?

What have been your past success(es)?

If this project is brand new, describe your history as a project leader working on projects of similar types.

Make the case for your project

This is the "why" section of the proposal. Write one to two paragraphs that contain the following (some may be more relevant to your specific project than others).

To help make your case, write responses to the following prompts:

Summarize the problem or issue your project addresses:

Discuss the mission and values that drive your project:

Describe the population that will benefit from your project:

Describe a need in your community that your project fulfils:

Statistics that support or illustrate this problem or issue:

Quotes from expert studies or articles that illustrate this problem or issue:

Discuss how your projects will address the problem or issue or fulfil a specific community need:

Why is now the optimum time for this problem or issue to be addressed or need to be fulfilled?

State your methods

This is the "how" section of the proposal. Write a paragraph about how you will achieve your goal(s) and objectives.

Answer the questions below to help clarify your methods:

What will happen between now and when the project is completed?

How do the actions you will take relate to the goal(s) and objectives you stated?

Timeline

This is the "when" section of your proposal.

List the tasks needed to achieve your proposal and how long they will take to complete

Task #1 (length, estimated completion date)

Task #2 (length, estimated completion date)

Task #3 (length, estimated completion date)

Grant application tracking calendar

To keep track of grants and awards you plan to apply for, create a calendar or spreadsheet. This will also help you stay aware of upcoming deadlines and prevent you from scrambling to apply at the last minute.

You can copy the template at http://microcosm.pub/qydj to use for your own purposes.

	Grant 1	Grant 2
Name of Funding Organization		
Organization Contact Name		
Contact Information		
Link to Application		
Materials Needed		
Deadline		
Date Applied		
Date Notified		
Accepted Y/N		
Notes		

Organizing Fundraising Events

Most of us have been to a benefit show, dance, dinner, potluck, picnic, auction, or walk-a-thon. These are all fundraising events in various guises. Organizing an event helps spread the word about your project, get more community members involved in supporting it, and bring people together in a way that is fun, social, and informative. However, organizing events is also a lot of work and can be very expensive, so think carefully before you decide to throw a fabulous party.

Events are a great opportunity to bring the community together around a DIY project. Enlist others to get involved in the project and to help you organize the event. Shannon Stratton, the Founder, and Executive and Creative Director of threewalls gallery in Chicago explains how she gets her core supporters involved in events, "I get people who care about us, who have a passion for the resource we have created and understand why we matter to ask others to give to us and get involved."

Reflect on the following to plan a great fundraising event:

What is the incentive that will get people to come out and spend their money?

Who is your audience for this event?

Time your fundraiser to an important "event" on the project's timeline.

- o *Are you launching or wrapping up an important phase of the project?*
- o *What is the newsworthy item that will make people excited about supporting your project at this time?*

How can you match the tone of your event to the project?

- o *For example, if you are organizing a campaign against police brutality, a carnival-style, burlesque fundraiser might not be the strongest fit, or maybe it would be if that's something your community would support*

How will the event raise money for your project or cause? List all the ways you can make money at the event

- o *For example, will you sell tickets, hold an auction, sell food, drinks, or fun products?*
- o *Be sure you publicize the event as a fundraiser, not just a fun party, and ensure guests are willing to open up their wallets and hearts to support your cause*

How much money do you have to spend on the event?

Where will you host the event? Do you have to rent the space?

Will the proposed venue be welcoming, accessible, and appealing to the community you want to attract to the event? Is it the right size and capacity for the event?

There are many practical and logistical elements of events to consider, when planning an event:

- Plan three to six months in advance

- Make a budget for your event

    o   Use the budgeting exercises in this workbook to help you

    o   Save your receipts so you can track costs and, potentially, write expenses off on your taxes

- Determine your entry price based on your budget

    o   Factor in overhead such as supplies, venue and equipment rental, and your time planning

    o   Ensure that your ticket price covers your expenses and raise money for your project

- Secure space, entertainment, and refreshments

- Publicize the event and sell tickets in advance

    o   Use the publicity planning exercises in this workbook to help you

- Collect email addresses from participants to stay in touch after the event

- After the event is over, thank everyone who attended (if possible) and helped you

- Analyze what worked well and what you would do differently next time

Event planning timeline checklist

Similar to the project planning timeline in section 1, adapt this timeline to your event's specific needs. This will ensure an organized event and prevent last minute event stress as much as possible.

Events work best when you plan them 3 - 6 months in advance, depending on the size of the event. Even for smaller events, it's important to secure your date in advance so you can properly promote it.

Event title:

Completion/launch date:

3 - 6 months in advance:

○   Set a goal for the event

○   Determine an ideal size for the event

○   Set a budget for the event

- ○ Choose a date and time for the event
- ○ Secure a venue for the event

1-3 months in advance:
- ○ Plan activities
- ○ Book speakers or entertainment
- ○ Order food or refreshments (or solicit donations for food and refreshments)
- ○ Set up ticketing or RSVP page
- ○ Publicize your event
- ○ Solicit help or volunteers for day-of
- ○ Plan decorations/decor
- ○ Make a list of all of the supplies you need

Week of event:
- ○ Reconfirm venue, food, and beverage orders
- ○ Reconfirm speakers and entertainment
- ○ Create a day-of logistics document to share with all entertainers and volunteers
- ○ Confirm day-of roles with all volunteers
- ○ Pick up decorations and supplies

Day of event:
- ○ Double check your logistics and reconfirm arrival time with entertainers, volunteers, and caterers
- ○ Arrive at the venue early to set up

◯ Check in with volunteers about roles and expectations

◯ Check all the technology you will use

◯ Conduct soundchecks with speakers and entertainers

◯ During the event check in with volunteers and ensure everything is going smoothly

◯ Take photos and/or video to post on social media

◯ Relax and enjoy

◯ Thank everyone for coming and for their help

Post event:

◯ Send a thank you email to all participants

  ◯ Include any necessary follow up information, upcoming events, or ways to get more involved or continue to support your project

◯ Send a thank you email or note to all volunteers

◯ Add all expenses and income to your event budget

  ◯ How much did you make in comparison to what you spent?

◯ Reflect on the following questions:

  ◯ What were the three most successful parts of this event? Why?

  ◯ What did not work about the event? Why?

  ◯ What did you learn that you will apply to the next event you plan?

Chapter Six Checklist

◯ Plan your fundraising strategy based on how what type of fundraising tactics are the best fit for your project

◯ Plan and launch a crowdfunding campaign

◯ Plan and launch a subscription to your project

◯ Research and apply for a grant

◯ Plan and host a fundraising event

BUSINESS STRUCTURE

L aunching a business, or turning your do-it-yourself project into a legal business, is your ticket to participate in the economy on your own terms. It allows you to build economic support for your vision and passion. Your project can be as creative, subversive, or as radical as you are and you want to build a framework that supports your work. When you take the do-it-yourself route, you are walking the path of an entrepreneur. Luckily, there are many resources available to you.

While these exercises are not a substitute for legal or financial advice (only a lawyer or accountant can give you that!), they will introduce you to the basic business structures, terminology, and resources you need to build a strong legal and logistical foundation for your project or business and help you assess what might be right for you.

Registering as a business can protect you, and the people you are collaborating with, from liability and ensures you have proper structures set up for record keeping, taxation, and governance. As you set your goals and timeline for your project work, registering as a business can be part of your overall plan, if it is applicable to your project.

Look into these organizations for resources, workshops and in-person consultations:

SCORE: a nonprofit organization dedicated to the education, support, and growth of fledgling small businesses. They offer free counseling and workshops for start-up businesses all across the country and have a wealth of templates and worksheets available online, including a guide to choosing a legal entity for your business.

The Small Business Administration offers well organized, clearly presented business resources that discuss considerations for eco-oriented business, nonprofit organizations, and startups with high growth potential. They also have specific resources for self-employed individuals, women and minority-owned businesses, and businesses run by people with disabilities. The SBA also includes guides and links to forms for how to incorporate.

Tips for Deciding on a Business Entity

When you know where you stand legally, you can create the groundwork for a sustainable project. Antonio Ramos of Brooklyn Soda Works said, "Put your project first and find a legal structure for your business that supports what you want to make." Consider these tips:

- Assess how each option for incorporations aligns with your project's goals, vision and mission

- Reach out to others with businesses similar to yours and ask them why they chose the entity they did and what their experience has been

- Choose your business entity carefully—changing it later can create a legal headache

- If incorporating with the help of a lawyer know what you need from them and what you can do yourself

Types of Business

The type of business entity you choose depends on your needs and goals. In the United States, there are several major types of business entities. When you are ready to choose a business entity, research what is available to you in your state. The Small Business Administration provides state-by-state information on legal incorporation. Depending on what state you are incorporating in, some forms may be legal and others may not be. In addition, the process of incorporation works slightly differently in each state.

Below are the basic entities that you will encounter, space to reflect on whether or not they may be a fit for you, and questions to ask a lawyer, business counselor, or accountant:

Sole Proprietorship: The most common business entity when you are starting a business on your own. Sole proprietorship gives you complete control and is easy to set up. However, it does not limit your liability, meaning that your company's liability is your own personal liability. The same goes for taxes—you file taxes for both your personal earnings and the business.

If your business has a name other than your own, you will need to file a "Doing Business As" or "DBA" with your county clerk for your new or "fictitious" business name. The Small Business Administration has a chart on their website that lists the requirements for registering your DBA in each state.

Pros of this business structure for you:

Cons:

Questions you have:

Limited Liability Corporation (LLC): This is another very common business structure and is a hybrid-legal structure that offers flexibility like a partnership, but protects the partners from liability like a corporation. LLCs can be owned by one or more people, and taxes are passed on to the owners of the LLC. Many filmmakers will create an LLC for their film to protect themselves from liability on their film shoots. The process of forming an LLC varies from state-to-state and LLCs are not legal in all states.

Pros of this business structure for you:

Cons:

Questions you have:

Partnership: If you are starting a business with two or more people who are contributing money, property and expertise, you are a partnership. There are several different types of partnerships with different requirements for taxation, liability and legal responsibility. Partners often have to pay taxes on the businesses profits and their personal profits, which can be very high. In addition, you want to ensure you have a legal agreement with your business partner that clearly outlines each of your responsibility, and liability, should any problems arise later.

Pros of this business structure for you:

Cons:

Questions you have:

Cooperative: Common in service providers, the retail industry, agricultural and even real-estate fields, cooperatives are owned and operated by a group of members who benefit from its profits and services. They have a board of directors that govern the co-op and members that have voting power to make decisions. Think about your local food or childcare co-op as an example. Co-ops are a democratic structure that requires you to create bylaws and a membership application.

Pros of this business structure for you:

Cons:

Questions you have:

Corporation: A corporation is a legal entity that is independent from its founders and is owned by its shareholders. The corporation, and not its shareholders, is held legally liable for its taxes, profits and debts. Depending on the type of corporation you form, such as a C-Corporation or S-Corporation, your business will pay taxes on an annual or quarterly schedule. Overall, corporations are the most expensive and complicated business entity to form.

Pros of this business structure for you:

Cons:

Questions you have:

Social Benefit Corporation (B Corporation): A relatively new corporate structure that uses for-profit models to address social and environmental issues. B Corps are certified by a nonprofit organization, B Lab, as adhering to certain environmental, labor, and social benefit standards. B Corps are not legal in all states. To create a B Corp, you must first incorporate using one of the structures above and then apply to B Lab for certification. B Corps aim to address the gap between for-profit and nonprofit legal entities.

Pros of this business structure for you:

Cons:

Questions you have:

Nonprofit: These organizations provide a public benefit and use their profits to improve their services. Because they are serving a charitable purpose they are exempt from taxation. Forming a nonprofit is a two-step process. First you must incorporate on the state level and then apply to the IRS for your federal, tax-exempt status. This status, called 501(c)(3) in the tax-code, enables individuals to receive a tax-deduction for giving to your organization and makes your nonprofit eligible for many grant programs. Nonprofits still must file their earnings with the IRS even though they are tax exempt and those taking a salary from nonprofits still must pay taxes on it.

Pros of this business structure for you:

Cons:

Questions you have:

Business creation checklist:

○ Choose a business entity

○ Select a business name

○ Incorporate and obtain an Employer Identification Number

• This is necessary for opening up a business bank account

- ○ State sales tax license (if selling goods)

- ○ Get a business license if necessary

- ○ Obtain the necessary insurance and permits

- ○ Write and sign contracts and memorandums of understanding your collaborators

Contract Basics

You've heard the expression "Get it in writing," and whether you have incorporated as a business or are just beginning to collaborate, a written agreement is essential. An agreement ensures that terms of your partnership are clear and that you all understand the roles and responsibilities you are taking on.

An agreement in writing is especially important when you are working with friends. Christen Carter, of Busy Beaver Buttons, advises that when working with friends, "Trade or give each other discounts on things that you don't do to earn your living, like business advice." Filmmaker William Badgley recommends, "When working with and negotiating with friends take care of the business aspects first. Then you know everything you need is in place and you can be social."

If you are collaborating with one person, a group or people, or between organizations, once you have decided on the terms of your collaboration, create a memorandum of understanding, or an MOU. An MOU lists the roles and responsibilities of each party involved. Each person signs and dates the completed memo. An MOU may not be legally binding, but it is an important document to have in order to clarify and refer back to what everyone is taking on.

Good contracts are good business. When you have a contract, you keep the relationship you have forged with a colleague, friend, or collaborator healthy. When you make a contract with a person or organization you are working with, it is an act of respect, empowerment and courtesy. A contract clearly spells out each party's obligations and responsibilities. It doesn't need to be written in fancy legal language, but must include the following to be considered valid within the United States:

- What the contract is offering
- What each party is expected to do or produce
- The obligation each has party has to another
- How payment or exchange will take place
- What will happen if each does not hold up their side of the bargain

Basic contract template

Please note: check with a lawyer before signing any contract or creating one of your own, the template below is to give you an idea of what a contract can include.

Legal address of party 1

Legal address of party 2

This contract is made on [date] between [name 1], of [legal address of name 1], and [name 2] of, [legal address of name 2].

The parties agree to the following terms and conditions:

1. This contract is valid until [date].
2. [Name 1] agrees to provide [Name 2] with the following [list goods or services that will be provided] on or by [date].
3. For [goods and services] [Name 2] will provide [Name 1] with [list payment amount here and the terms of payment].
4. If [the goods and services are not delivered] [Name 1] will have the right to [what will Name 1 do].
5. List any other terms or conditions or consequences if they are not upheld
6. Both parties agree to the terms and conditions mentioned in this contract.

Name 1: Signature and date

Name 2: Signature and date

For basic contracts, such as between buyers and sellers, or freelancers, you can often find a wider array of standard language templates online. To enter into a contract both parties must be over 18 and do so of their own freewill and the activity the contract covers must be legal. In addition, each party must gain something from the relationship. If one party benefits and the other does not, the exchange is considered a gift, and doesn't require a contract.

Empower yourself to understand and be vocal about your needs whether you are creating a contract or receiving one. Review your contract carefully and make sure you understand each clause. Ask if you do not. If you are entering into a complicated legal agreement, such as a contract with a record company or a film distributor, review your contract with a lawyer who specializes in these areas. The money you will pay them will save you heartache, pain and, in the long run, money.

Healthy Collaboration

"Do It Yourself" doesn't mean "Do It Alone"—projects can benefit immensely from collaboration with others. It takes time, planning, and effort to build successful collaborations and rewarding partnerships that help your project grow or your business run effectively. Collaborations must be carefully cultivated and nurtured to be sustainable.

In collaboration or barter situations, be cautious about mixing friendships and business. You may find it's easier to trade business advice, but avoid offering discounts or free services for things that directly impact your business revenue.

Guidelines for healthy collaboration:

- Work with people whose talents and skills complement yours

- Be honest about your strengths and weaknesses

- Communicate your needs, expectations, hopes, and fears

- Be clear about what you want out of the collaboration

- Define each partners' roles in writing

- Give back as much as you are getting out of the collaboration

- Check in with your partners and reassess the collaboration regularly

I have / I need

This simple exercise can help you hone in on what you need from a collaboration and what you can offer in return. Under "I have" write down the skills, resources, and anything else you can offer to others. Under "I need" write down what you need to continue to grow your project and make it successful. This will help you hone in on your strengths and where you need help from others.

I have:

I need:

Define your collaboration parameters

Similar to the "plan to barter better" exercise in the budgeting and finance chapter, getting the expectations for your collaboration in writing can clarify your needs and expectations.

With your collaborator(s) discuss:

- What are your motivations for working together?

- What do you both hope to get out of your collaboration?

- What specific skills and/or resources will you each be bringing/offering to the project?

- How much time are you realistically giving to the project on a weekly or monthly basis?

- When do you estimate the project will be complete?

- How and when will you end the partnership—how will you decide on that together?

Get it in writing

Once you've discussed the expectations and hopes for your collaboration, outline the relationship in writing. Even if you are entering into a collaboration with a friend, defining and documenting the parameters of your collaboration will help you keep both your business and friendship relationships healthy and keep a boundary between the two.

Use the following prompts to draft a collaboration between two (or more) partners:

Partner 1 responsibilities:

Partner 2 responsibilities:

We commit to working on this project _____ hours a week

We commit to checking in every _____ weeks

We will complete or reassess the project by _____
[date]

How we will split/share revenue:

How we will split/share responsibility for project expenses:

Check in with your collaborators

Working with other people can be rewarding, motivating, and exciting, and also emotionally draining and challenging. Having regular check-ins can normalize the reflection process and help you address any differences in opinion and expectation before they flare up.

Decide on a regular check in time with your collaborators and schedule them in advance. Reflect on these questions to prepare for your check-ins:

- This is what I have been able to accomplish:

- These aspects of the project are working for me:

- I need:

- I'm struggling with:

- I'd like to adjust:

You may find after working with someone for a set period of time that you are no longer a good match due to changing professional or personal priorities. It's okay to part ways—stay honest and transparent and honor your collaboration agreement as much as possible as you negotiate your changing relationship.

Chapter Seven Checklist

○ Determine the best legal structure for your project to protect you and your collaborators from liability and ensure you have proper structures set up for record keeping, taxation, and governance

○ Practice writing contracts, including MOUs, to garner healthy collaboration, articulate the expectations around people's work, and have systems of accountability in place, just in case

○ Define your guidelines for collaboration

BUILDING A DIY LIFE

When you embark on a do-it-yourself project you seize the opportunity to create your life how you want it. Building a DIY life is a process that takes time and conscious effort. You can empower yourself to develop healthy work habits, create a lifestyle that nurtures your project, build collaborations with other do-it-yourselfers that are productive and inspiring, and participate in a strong, supportive community.

Once you have gotten a handle on the practical and logistical aspects of your project you can figure out how to integrate it into the rest of your life and make your vision a reality. This chapter covers how to manage your work habits, how to stay motivated through challenging times, strategies for growing your business while staying DIY, and how to productively and creative work with other people to create a thriving do-it-yourself community.

Nurture Healthy Work Habits

"When you take on a do-it-yourself project in that moment you are deciding your own future," said filmmaker and musician William Badgley.

Taking your project to the next level requires organization and hard work. Finding a balance between procrastination and working so hard on your project you lose perspective requires self-knowledge and careful balancing. You need to know yourself very well to build a successful DIY project. Use these exercises to assess your work habits and skill sets to see where you might need to make a change to achieve greater success.

Understand your strengths, challenges, and opportunities

Take some time to do the following exercises and try to approach them curiosity, self-compassion, and an open mind. Growing a DIY business is also a personal growth project and that will mean stretching yourself personally and growing your self-awareness.

Assess and identify your strengths

Sometimes it helps to have an outside perspective to help you see into yourself. While there are endless personality tests you can take online, two of the most helpful are either the Gallup StrengthsFinder test (which costs about $20) or the free High5 test. These tests help you identify the top personality traits that you bring to your projects, business, and interactions with others.

After you've taken one of these tests, reflect on the following questions:

Were you surprised by the results? Why or why not?

How do you think these traits have contributed to the success of your project so far?

What strengths might you look for in project partners to complement your own?

Is there anything you can change about your project plan or approach that can make even better use of your strengths?

Conduct a personal SWOC analysis

Once you understand your strengths, it's time to look at your project more holistically. Traditionally businesses use something called a "SWOT" analysis, which stands for "strengths, weaknesses, opportunities, and threats," to assess where they stand relative to others in their markets. However, "threats" is too competitive and negative for our purposes, so we're substituting "challenges."

To conduct a SWOC analysis, make a list of your strengths, weaknesses, opportunities, and challenges when it comes to your business:

My strengths are:

1.

2.

3.

4.

5.

My weaknesses and where I have room to improve are:

1.

2.

3.

4.

5.

The opportunities I have to grow my project/business are:

1.

2.

3.

4.

5.

The challenges I'm currently facing are:

1.

2.

3.

4.

5.

Reflect on the following questions:

How can I leverage my strengths to take advantage of the opportunities I identified?

What else do I need to better take advantage of the opportunities I identified?

How do my strengths also contribute to my weaknesses?

Break the weaknesses into two categories:

An opportunity to learn or improve a skill:

A chance to hire or collaborate with someone who is really good at this:

What do you need to transform challenges into opportunities?

What do the challenges you're encountering tell you about what you might need to do differently in your business?

What are three actionable next steps you can take to take advantage of these opportunities or address the challenges you identified?

1.

2.

3.

Time Tracker (also find at microcosm.pub/gydj)

TIME	MONDAY	TUESDAY	WEDNESDAY	THURSDAY	FRIDAY	SATURDAY	SUNDAY

Understand Your Work Habits

It can be easy to feel like you need to be working and thinking about your project all the time, and that time is one of your most scarce resources. These exercises will help you understand how you are using the time you have and identify opportunities to work more efficiently to grow as a creative professional.

Understand your time management: Track your time

When you are balancing your project with another job, taking care of your life, and taking care of yourself, it can be easy to feel like you don't have enough time to do everything you need to do. To better figure out how to prioritize your time, and adjust as necessary, start by understanding how you are spending your time.

Spend one week tracking your time in 30 minute increments. You can use the chart on the previous pages, make notes in a notebook or on your phone, or use a time tracking app—whatever is easiest for you.

Once you've spent a week tracking your time, look at your chart and reflect:

What surprised you about how you spend your time?

Based on what you see, how do you want to adjust how you spend your time?

What could you spend less time on?
For example, spending time on your phone or social media, watching TV

How could you use your time more effectively to free up more time to work on your project?

For example, meal prep once or twice a week to cut down on cooking and clean up time

When do you work most effectively?

For example, morning, middle of the day, evening

Look at your time tracker and schedule and set aside 2 - 3 blocks of time a week during the time you work most effectively that you can dedicate to your project or creative practice.

Time block 1:

Time block 2:

Time block 3:

Block these times off in your calendar and do not schedule anything else during them.

Try the "pomodoro" technique for time management

This popular technique is great if you have a hard time sitting down to work in a focused and productive manner, or breaking through feelings of overwhelm and resistance to starting a project or your daily work. It's named after a tomato-shaped kitchen timer (a *pomodoro* in Italian).

Try it!

- Set a timer for 25 minutes

- Work continuously for that 25 minutes—no breaks, no checking the internet or your phone, no going to the bathroom, or getting a drink (unless it's an emergency!)

- When the timer rings take a 5 minute break to do whatever you want

- Set the timer for 25 minutes again and repeat

You may find that once you get into a "flow" and break through your resistance you'll want to work through the timer. This is great, but taking breaks is also important for keeping your mind fresh.

Understand your planning style

Reflect on the following questions. If you are not sure, think of how you have planned and implemented your plan for your project so far.

How do you approach a big project?
Do you jump in and start working right away, take the time to plan, or procrastinate?

What parts of the planning process do you struggle with or frustrate you? Why?

What is a different way you could approach the planning process to ease these frustrations?

To help ease any planning anxiety you may feel, revisit the goal and action item setting exercises in section 1. Then plan and do one task every day for a week to help you move forward towards your goal in an organized fashion.

Exercise: Rethink your to do list

To do lists can be extremely helpful, but can easily become sprawling and feel overwhelming because you can continuously add to them. Instead of a never ending to-do list, try to following:

- Write down the goal you want to accomplish in a specific amount of time. For example a week.

- Each day, write down the tasks you want to accomplish

- Now prioritize the three most important tasks

- Concentrate on getting those three tasks done each day

Understand your organizational style

Keeping your workspace organized is crucial to keeping your sanity as you grow your project or business. While decluttering may seem like a current fad, studies do show that a clean, clear workspace lowers stress and is better for your productivity and mental health. Especially when you have limited time to work on a project, keeping your workspace and tasks organized can mean that when you do have time to work you can get right into it.

On a scale of 1 to 5, how organized are you?

1.	2.	3.	4.	5.
Extremely disorganized	Disorganized	More-or-less organized	Organized	Extremely organized

Reflect: What is your biggest challenge when it comes to organization? *Messy workspace? Not a clear place to put everything? Too much stuff?*

Now that you know what you might need to tackle, take the following steps to organize your workspace:

- Get rid of anything you don't use or need
    - Be honest with yourself: This includes things you "might use someday" that you have been hanging on to for years
    - Divide what you are getting rid of into piles of trash, recycle, donante, and sell and then actually get them out of your house or workspace
- Organize the items you are keeping into what you use regularly and what you only use occasionally
- For the items you use regularly, find a "home" for each of them that is in easy reach
- For items you use less often, group them together in like categories
- Store them in a place that's easy to find and if you put them in boxes, label each box
- Get in the habit of putting things back in their place each time you use them
- Regularly declutter your workspace so cleaning it doesn't become overwhelming

Understand your communication style

Bringing a creative project to life and building a DIY business centers around your relationships and communication with others. Understanding how you communicate, and what you need to work on, can help strengthen your communication and business skills.

On a scale of 1 to 5, 1 being "extremely uncomfortable" and 5 being "extremely comfortable, rate the following statements about your communication style. Think of the numbers in the following way:

1 Extremely uncomfortable

2 Uncomfortable

3 I'm okay at it

4 Comfortable

5 Extremely comfortable

I am able to clearly communicate my needs and ask others for help:

1   —   2   —   3   —   4   —   5

My answer is because . . .

I am comfortable negotiating when it comes to money, obligations, or responsibility:

1   —   2   —   3   —   4   —   5

My answer is because . . .

I am comfortable with receiving feedback:

1   —   2   —   3   —   4   —   5

My answer is because . . .

I am comfortable with setting my boundaries and saying "no" when something is not in line with my goals and values, or I don't have the energy:

1   —   2   —   3   —   4   —   5

My answer is because . . .

Based on your answers above, what are some communication skills you feel you need to strengthen?

Communicating clearly can be intimidating, especially for those of us who have been taught by our families or by dominant culture to be "people pleasers" and put others' needs in front of our own. Committing to unifying your DIY lifestyle and your creative projects also means committing to honoring, and asserting, your needs, passions, and boundaries.

To help you get what you need, complete or edit these phrases to fit your specific context and practice saying them out loud until you feel comfortable (or at least, not terrified!).

Asking for help:

I need help with _____ . Could you help me?

Right now, I need_____ in order to _____ .

If you could help me complete_____ , it would really help me focus on other pressing issues.

Negotiating and talking about money:

My rate is_____ [amount] for_____
_____ [amount of time or project].

My price is set based on_____ [market/the going rate/my research]. This is the going rate for/ this is a good value for_____ .

Tell me what you need and how you think I could help.

What is most important to you?

My top priorities are_____ .
How will _____ [what they are offering] fit?

Let me take a few days to consider what you are offering.

Giving and receiving feedback

The most effective feedback is actionable, specific, and kind, or ASK for short. Giving "kind" feedback doesn't mean "being nice." The more actionable and specific feedback is, the kinder it is. Often we receive feedback such as, "It's good" or, "This didn't work for me," which is too vague to be actionable.

Use these questions to ask for actionable, specific feedback:

What was your favorite part of _____ ?

What was most effective about _____ ?

What is one way this product/experience could be improved?

Receiving feedback

Thank you for your feedback. I'd love to learn more about _____
_____[any part of their feedback that wasn't specific or clear]?

I appreciate you taking the time to tell me. Could you be more specific about
_____[anything vague or unclear]?

Thank you so much for letting me know. Your response means a lot to me. What
is one thing that could make _____
_____[your product or experience] even better?

Setting boundaries:

No.

No, thank you.

I can't do that right now.

That's not what I had in mind.

That doesn't work for me.

Right now I'm focused on _____and this doesn't fit in with
my current priorities.

Perspective, Self-Care, and Burnout

Keeping your project in perspective can ensure that you keep it creative, fun, and rewarding, while also taking care of yourself. The exercises in this section will help you practice self-care by reconnecting with your mission and values, and setting strong boundaries between your project and the rest of your life. Creating harmony between your project and other life interests and obligations is no easy task, but an important one for the long term sustainability of your project and your own health.

Reconnect with your vision, values, and mission

Your vision, values, and mission are the guides for your project. Taking time to reconnect with them is a way to care for yourself and the health of your project. When you take time to understand how your vision, values, and mission are driving and anchoring your project, you can feel more in touch with the deeper purpose of your project, and make focused decisions in line with your values.

Reflect on your success so far

As you work on your project, your vision of success will evolve. It's important to be clear about what you are hoping to achieve, so look back to the notes you took after your "envisioning success" daydream/meditation and/or take a look at your vision board.

Respond to the following prompts:

What parts of this vision have you achieved?

How did "success" look or feel different than you originally imagined?

What about this vision of success still feels relevant and true to you?

How can it evolve next?

Success meditation

Set aside half an hour or more and settle into a quiet place, either sitting or lying down comfortably (but not so comfortable you'll fall asleep!).

- Close your eyes or keep them open but softly focused.

- Take deep breaths to center yourself.

- Remember, during this process, nothing is "right" or "wrong"—it's about letting your mind wander enough so that you can connect with your deeper visions and desires.

- Once you feel centered and relaxed, imagine that your project is finished and it has been successful.

- What have you created?

- How is this different from your original vision of success?

- What did you need to get here that you might not have thought about before?

- How do you feel in your body?

Write down your reimagined vision of success here, in your journal, on sticky notes or note cards, or make a new vision board (refer to the first section for step-by-step instructions).

Complete this sentence:

Success to me now looks like...

Revisit your values

Return to the 6 to 8 "north star" values that you defined at the beginning of your project. For each value write, reflect on the following questions. If you find that some of the values you defined are no longer a fit for the project, reflect on whether you need to revisit and redefine your core values.

Value #1:
My project embodies this value by:

I could bring this value into my project more fully by:

Value #2:
My project embodies this value by:

I could bring this value into my project more fully by:

Value #3:

My project embodies this value by:

I could bring this value into my project more fully by:

Value #4:

My project embodies this value by:

I could bring this value into my project more fully by:

Value #5:

My project embodies this value by:

I could bring this value into my project more fully by:

Value #6:

My project embodies this value by:

I could bring this value into my project more fully by:

Value #7:
My project embodies this value by:

I could bring this value into my project more fully by:

Value #8:
My project embodies this value by:

I could bring this value into my project more fully by:

Reconnect with your mission

Revisit your mission statement and write it here:

How does your project reflect your mission statement so far?

How does re-reading your mission statement make you feel? Does it still feel relevant? Why or why not?

What else do you need to bring your mission statement to life?

Does your mission statement need to evolve to continue to be a fit with your project? What have you learned that is driving that evolution?

If your mission statement needs to evolve, revisit the exercise in section one and then write your updated mission statement here:

Reflect on Your Goals and Timeline

Your goals will evolve with your project. Set a time, whether monthly or quarterly, to check in with your goals and timeline and revise them as necessary. Successful creative people and projects are adaptable—they are able to adjust to changing timelines and circumstances without losing their vision or focus.

Is your project going according to plan? Why or why not?

Which goals have you achieved?

How did achieving those goals make you feel?

What did you learn from them?

Which remaining goals still feel relevant?

Which goals do you need to revise based on the current state of your project?

Is your timeline realistic based on your other life obligations?

Look at your time tracking exercise—are you spending enough time for yourself, friends, and family outside of your project and other work obligations?

Check in with Your Passion

One of the tricky elements of being driven by passion is that it can ebb and flow. This is natural for creative people. Like any relationship, as you get to know your project better and spend more time with it, the type of passion you feel for it may change. This is perfectly normal. Checking in with your passion and the type of energy your project brings to your life can give you important information about what's working and what you might want to change.

Reflect on the following questions:

What about your project do you love? Why do you love that part of it?

What are the good things, expected or unexpected, that your project brings to your life?

How do you feel when you work on your project?

How would you like to feel when you work on your project?

What practice, ritual, or habit could you bring to your project to reconnect with your passion and feel more of what you "want" to feel when you work? *For example, take breaks every hour for a 5 minute dance party, meditate before sitting down to work, lighting a candle at your workstation*

Set Boundaries Between Business and Life

The nature of a DIY project is that you take it on and do much of it yourself. While your project may be a close reflection of your passions, values, and personality, it is not the entirety of your being. Creating healthy boundaries between your work and the rest of your life can ensure you are staying grounded and can avoid burnout. Differentiating between your project and yourself can help you keep your project in perspective when it gets challenging or you feel overwhelmed.

Time block your project

Especially when you are working through something challenging or frustrating it can be easy to get sucked into your project and feel like you have to keep working on it, no matter what. Sometimes hammering away at a problem or challenge, or just feeling like we should always be working on our projects, doesn't actually help them advance and leads to frustration and burnout.

Instead, try "time blocking" which simply means choosing an amount of time to work on a particular aspect of your project. For example, choose to work on a specific challenge for 30 minutes and then take a break. You might find that the solution comes to you when you rest your mind and focus on something else.

Try it!

- Set aside 3-4 dedicated blocks of time a week to work on your project

- Choose what you will work on during each block

- You could even use the pomodoro method to further divide the blocks and focus your tasks further

- When the time you have set aside is over, stop working

Set aside time to step away from your project

Remember: You are not your project. Find time to nurture goals and passions that are separate from your project.

Try it!

Write 2 -3 goals that are not related to your project:

1.

2.

3.

Next, consult your time tracking log and find two blocks of time a week that you can dedicate to these goals. You could use this time for taking a class unrelated to your project, spending time with friends or family, going for a walk, or doing whatever you want!

Only ask for feedback from people whose opinion and judgement you trust

When we are excited about working on a project it can be tempting to talk about it with everyone who will listen and ask them for their opinion. Be careful with this! Your interactions with others may become too one-sided and you may end up with feedback that is neither actionable, specific, nor relevant to your project. Instead, ask for feedback from specific peers who have expertise in an area of your project and keep casual conversations casual.

Try it!

- Make a list of 3 to 5 peers you respect who you would like to receive feedback from

- Reach out and ask them to give you feedback and offer to give feedback on a project of theirs in return

- For others, write or revisit your one line description of your project and practice saying it, "I'm working on . . ." and then moving on in conversation

Take time off

When you are involved in a DIY project, you set your schedule and the pace of your work. This means you are also responsible for finding time when you can step away from your project to rest, reflect, and recharge. While it can be tempting to keep grinding away on your project, studies show that taking time off from work helps with creativity and productivity.

Try it!

- Choose one evening a week when you do not schedule anything related to your project (or anything at all, if possible)

- Pick one weekend a month to do something fun

- Schedule at least 2 weeks off a year from your project (and full time job or additional work, if you can) so you can fully relax and recharge

Sustainable Growth

As your project grows, you will inevitably learn lessons through experience, but you can also build in reflections to make sure sustainable growth is part of your work process.

Take care of your customers

Your customers are extremely valuable members of your community. They have supported you financially by buying your product or services. Take time to thank them and learn more about them.

Be responsive

- Set aside time each day to respond to customer questions, feedback, and inquiries

- If you receive negative feedback, ask for more explanation so you can understand how to rectify the situation

Learn more about your customers

- Use data and analytics on your website or online store to understand where most of your customers are coming from

- Ask for feedback as a follow up to each order you receive

- Create a short survey to share with your customers once or twice a year

Thank and celebrate your customers

- Consider creating a special product or discount just for your most loyal supporters

- Thank them regularly in your email newsletters and on social media

  - Share and repost any posts where they mention you as well

- Create a special event, like a workspace tour or small reception, to say thank you to your customers

Sample customer survey

Customize this sample customer survey to learn more about your customers. You can put this survey on your website or send it out in your email newsletter:

I'd love to learn more about you so I can create new products/services that you'll love and will help you! Please take a few minutes to fill this out.

Where do you live?

Age range? [list a range of ages]

Social media handle:

How did you hear about us?

What is your favorite product/service? Why?

What else would you be interested in seeing me make/offer that would be useful to you?

Where do you learn about new products/services like this?

What could I do better?

What is the best way I can thank and recognize your support?

Know when to bring in help

As your business grows or your project matures, you may find that you are stretched thin and that it makes sense to hire someone for tasks you used to take care of yourself in order to focus on growing the business. You may also find you need the advice and guidance of someone with specific professional expertise, such as a lawyer or accountant, to help you take the next step.

Use this exercise to check in with yourself and to identity where you might need to bring in extra help:

My favorite tasks for my project or business are:

I can't stand doing:

Tasks that can only be done by me include:

I need professional help with:

You might find that, for example, only you can come up with new products for your business and craft specific pieces, but you need help putting together and shipping orders. You might consider hiring someone a few hours a week to help with packaging and shipping, for example.

Write a sample job description to find someone to help you with your project. Outline the specific requirements and responsibilities:

Check in and reflect on your growth

What is driving you towards success? How is it making you feel? Answer the questions below to check in with yourself and ensure your motivation is coming from a healthy, sustainable place.

I'm motivated to keep my project growing because:

My motivation aligns with my values, vision, and mission because:

If your motivation does not align with your values, vision, and mission, how can you become better aligned?

My level of commitment to my project feels (circle one):

High   Medium   Low

Why?

The energy and time my project requires to keep growing feels (circle one):

Too much   Just right   Too low

In 6 months I want to feel _____ about my project.

I need the following resources to get there:

Chapter Eight Checklist

◯ Support your work by developing healthy boundaries between your working life and your personal life

◯ Identify your strengths, weaknesses, opportunities, and challenges to understand ways you can improve your focus, strengthen your communication, develop boundaries, and ask for help

◯ Develop strategies to keep yourself accountable to your working timeline

◯ Take time to reflect on your values so you can live and work in alignment

- Meditate on your vision of success, revisit your goals and adjust them if necessary, and check in with your energy level and passion

◯ Develop sustainable growth by tuning into yourself

PREPARE FOR FULL-TIME DIY

I f your project is gathering momentum and your success is growing, you may be considering whether you want to make the leap to making your project your full time job. Before you jump head first into full time DIY, use the following prompts and exercises to assess what makes sense for you and make a transition plan to ease into a sustainable, successful DIY life.

Your Personal Life

Create your ideal schedule

Revisit the "Understanding your work habits" section. Are there any habits you need to address around timeliness or self-discipline before you make the leap?

Based on what you know about your work style, most effective working times, and your other life obligations, set up an ideal "work week" schedule including creative time, administrative time, client meetings, and networking with your community. Be realistic as possible about the time each activity will take.

Also take into account time to eat, exercise, sleep, spend time with friends and family, and do activities not related to your project.

	Day 1	Day 2	Day 3	Day 4	Day 5
Early morning					
Morning					
Afternoon					
Evening					
Night					

After mapping out your idea work week, what surprises you about how much time is, or is not, available?

Connect With Your Community

Embracing a "do it yourself" life doesn't mean being isolated or doing everything alone. One of the biggest strengths of DIY is the community around it. Follow the steps below to strengthen your community and broaden your support network as your transition to a full time creative business owner.

Reflect on the following questions:

Do you need a community around you when you work?

How has your community supported your project so far?

How might they support it in the future?

List five places where your community gathers and where you can meet and network with other people similar to you (these could be in person or online locations):

Connect with experienced community members

From your community identity 3 to 5 people who have had a similar trajectory to you and run a full time creative business or make a living off their creative work. Write their names here:

1.

2.

3.

4.

5.

Write them a short email, introducing yourself, and asking them to coffee, and letting them know you'd love to learn about their experience and process making the transition to full time creative work. Keep the tone light and polite. Ask about their story, as opposed to business advice. People love talking about themselves! If they agree to meet you, send them a thank you note.

If you really clicked with them, consider setting up regular meetings or coffee dates to keep you motivated, share advice, and so they can serve as a mentor.

Communicate about your transition plan

Planning on launching your project full time is a big deal! Refer to the email newsletter and social media planning section to plan an email newsletter and social media posts to let your network know about your transition.

Send personal emails or call your closest family, friends, and supporters and let them know that you would be honored if they bought your products, considered hiring you, or helped spread the word about the services you have available.

List five to ten people you want to personally reach out to in order to tell them about your new job and professional direction:

1.

2.

3.

4.

5.

Celebrate Your New DIY Life!

Working for yourself at a career you made yourself is a big deal! Take time to plan a celebration that marks your debut into full time DIY. This need not be an expensive blow out, but something to acknowledge and mark your new professional direction.

Your Professional Life

Planning on making most, or a significant portion, of your living from your DIY project is a big leap, so this is the time to get very real about your finances before anything takes you by surprise.

Answering the following questions will help you know if you are financially ready to transition to full time DIY.

Add up your monthly business expenses, including studio rent, website hosting, creative and office supplies, and postage:

Add up your monthly living expenses, including rent, bills, groceries, and transportation:

Add up your personal expenses that might be considered "optional," such as meals out and entertainment:

If you had to cut back on your monthly spending, where could you spend less?

Is your lifestyle in line with running a small business?

Assess your savings account—some financial planners recommend having 3 to 6 months of living expenses saved up as an emergency fund. How long will it take to save this buffer of funds?

Meet with an accountant to discusses:

- Taxes: will you have to file taxes quarterly? How much of your income should you set aside for taxes? Most recommend at least 30%

- Write offs: what kind of documentation do you need to file your taxes properly and what from your business can you write off?

- Health insurance: If you are no longer receiving health benefits from an employer and need to purchase your own insurance, research the options available in your state. How does this impact your expenses?

- Workspace: What is the ideal workspace for you as your business grows? Research spaces and ask community members to price out what is available in your area.

Do You Really Need to Make a Living from Your Project?

The great thing about a DIY life is that you can decide how to set it up. You need not choose between "full time job" and "full time DIY," but can find a combination of making money that works for you. There is no right or wrong way to DIY!

Maybe you find a part-time job that gives you some financial stability, but frees your schedule up to work on your project. Maybe you take on freelance clients using a skill you are particularly good at, like copy editing or book keeping, while also working on your project.

If you realize you need to have a full time job, perhaps you could consider transitioning jobs into something more aligned with your project or that will give you specific skills or experience that will be helpful as a creative business owner. Or maybe you realize you want a fulltime job that has nothing to do with your creative project because you want to create a boundary between the two.

Use the questions below to reflect on your motivations and brainstorm different ways to support yourself financially.

Skills I have that people value or will pay for (for example, copy editing, translation, graphic design, web development, accounting):

My motivations for transitioning away from full time work:

List 3 to 5 strategies or opportunities to earn income outside of your DIY project:

1.

2.

3.

4.

5.

Which one of those would you prefer to do?

Which one would be easiest to start?

Prepare to Transition from Your Employer

If you have a job, talk about your decision with your employer and ensure that you leave your job as professionally, politely, and with as much goodwill as possible. You never know when you will work together again and in what capacity

Set a meeting to discuss:

- Departure date—give as much notice as possible

- The possibility of continuing to work part-time if you are interested or until your role is filled

- Transition plan

Chapter Nine Checklist

◯   Create a calendar that proportionately dedicates time to work, taking care of yourself, family and friend time, and relaxing!

◯   Tap into your network to get perspective on the growth of your project relative to similar projects

- You can also ask for opportunities, access to resources, or for them to spread the word about your flourishing passion

◯   Consider your financial landscape beyond this project to determine if you can live off your DIY project full-time

REFLECT, REASSESS, AND STAY MOTIVATED

When you build a creative, do-it-yourself life, project, or business, you empower yourself to create the life you want. You are sending a message that you believe in yourself and a creative vision and you're willing to go against the grain of what is "normally" expected of your work, life, and career. Not everyone will necessarily share that vision and you will encounter resistance along the way. In order to stay motivated about your project, take time to reassess it honestly, and define and celebrate what it brings to your life.

Take time to acknowledge your creativity and your own needs. Justin Hocking warns, "There can be a martyr syndrome in the DIY community and people can fall into the trap of, "I am doing it for the good of the community," but you should think about how you design your job and your life around your own creative work."

Celebrate Your Success

We can get so wrapped up in pushing ourselves forward and growing our projects that we can forget to pause and celebrate our successes. Celebrating your successes can help remind you how far you've come and help you feel good about all you have accomplished.

Your successes need not be only the most visible, successful parts of your project. You can also celebrate accomplishing tasks like creating your budget or launching a new website or email newsletter.

Choose 3 project milestones you want to celebrate:

1.

2.

3.

Brainstorm ways to celebrate those milestones below. They could be something like making a special meal for those who have helped you get there or going on a trip to the beach or a museum.

Stop/Start/Continue Exercise

This exercise is a simple way for you to assess what is, and is not, working for your project. Use it throughout your project to help you reflect and change course as necessary.

You can do this exercise in this workbook, on large pieces of chart paper on the wall, or with post-it notes. Be as honest as possible—write down each item without judgement. This is also a great exercise to do to check in with collaborators.

I'd like to start doing:

I'd like to stop doing:

I'd like to continue doing:

Once you have written down what you wish to stop, start, and continue, write your next steps here:

Connect with Your Creativity

Sometimes in the day-to-day work of cultivating and growing your project you can lose contact with your creativity. Staying closer to the creativity that drives you can also help you stay motivated with your project.

Write your responses to the prompts below or in your journal:

I feel most creative when...

I get excited when I work on...

When I work on my project I want to feel...

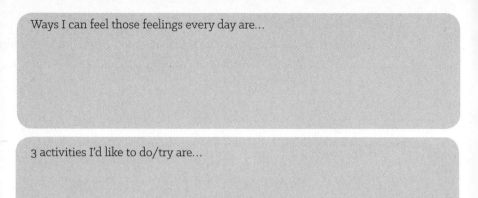

Ways I can feel those feelings every day are...

3 activities I'd like to do/try are...

Think of a creative pursuit you'd like to do that has nothing to do with your project, like sketching, dancing, or singing:

Schedule time to do that at least 20 minutes a day for a week.

After a week, how do you feel? How do you want to change your way of working based on that feeling?

Envision the Future

This exercise is a version of designer and educator Debbie Millman's "Remarkable Life" exercise, which she learned from her mentor, designer Milton Glaser. Take as much time as you need for this exercise, I recommend several hours, if possible.

- For this exercise, you'll need a journal and a writing utensil

- Sit comfortably and connect with your breath

- Keeping your focus soft, take a few deep breaths

- When you feel calm and centered, imagine this very same day, 5 years in the future

- Where are you? What are you doing? How do you feel? Who are you with? Let the vision come to you without judgement

- Stretch yourself to dream and imagine as audaciously as possible

- Now, spend as long as you need writing about your day from the moment you wake up and get out of bed until the moment you go to sleep.

    - Be as detailed as possible: What kind of beverage do you drink in the morning? What is the light in your bedroom like? How do your sheets feel? Your clothes? How is your workspace set up? Are you working at home or do you travel there? How does each task you take on make you feel?

- Don't limit or edit yourself

- Keep writing until you can't think of anything else to write

Read what you have written back. How do you feel? What can you start doing now to bring about this feeling? Read your "ideal day" back to yourself at least once a year. When you do, reflect, what still feels true? What is already true?

Find an Accountability Buddy

Working with someone else can help you stay motivated, reflect on what you have accomplished, and refocus when you need. Meeting regularly with your accountability partner can help you tackle your project bit by bit.

To find an accountability buddy:
- Identify someone with a goal or project similar to yours

- Be sure they are someone you trust and respect

- They need not be your best and closest friend

- Define the terms of your relationship, including how often you want to meet

- Use the healthy collaboration worksheet to help draft an agreement

During your accountability meetings review:

- Your goals for the past month

- Something that happened that you are proud of

- What worked, what didn't work, and why

- Your goals for the upcoming month

- Any challenge you need help thinking through

You may find it helpful to set a timer, so that you each have an equal time to share and get advice.

Chapter Ten Checklist

◯ Stop and appreciate the work you have put into your project thus far, celebrate yourself!

◯ Tune into your creative energy

- Ask yourself if and how you want to continue your work, and be honest with yourself

◯ Envision yourself in 5 years: who are you, what are you doing, what does your life feel like?

◯ Find an accountability buddy: a like-minded person to review your progress with, who will give you constructive and unbiased feedback

RECOGNIZING YOUR PROJECT'S LIFECYCLE

CONSIDERATIONS FOR ENDING OR CHANGING

Change happens. When you take a risk to bring a creative project to life, you are also embarking on a journey and embracing growth. Outside of yourself, the economy, technology, and culture is constantly shifting and changing. Some projects are finite and come to a natural close, while others rely on a conscious decision and actions to wind them down. While your feelings about your project will constantly evolve, if you find that your project is no longer serving your mission, vision, values, and goals, it may be time to end or radically change it.

When considering ending a project, take time to reflect on the following questions:

Is your project a source of joy and motivation? Why or why not?

Has the reason you started the project changed?

Is this project still aligned with your goals, values, vision, and mission?

Is the project still relevant to the community or culture that it serves?

Have the needs and interests of project partners, community members, or collaborators shifted?

Is the project no longer financially sustainable—is it losing money or are you going into debt?

Think about how your reasons for continuing your project have changed. In reflecting, you might find an alternative way to bring the feelings and activities your project provides you into your life.

I started this project because ...

I continue to work on this project because...

If I stopped working on this particular project I could still use the skills I have learned and connect to the community I have built by...

Check in with Your Feelings

Another way to assess whether you should continue a project is to check in with your feelings. This is a version of "listening to your gut." As you check in with your feelings, let them arise without judgement.

Close your eyes and take some deep, centering breaths. When you feel focused and calm, reflect on the following questions.

When I think about my project I feel . . .

When I think about stopping this project, I feel . . .

When I think about continuing this project, I feel . . .

If you find that you feel a heaviness, burden, anxiety, or panic when you think about your project, and relief when you think about stopping your project, it might be time to consider letting it go.

Recognize Your Accomplishments

Our culture tends to only recognize and celebrate a very narrow version of success. However, when you embrace DIY, you also empower yourself to define success on your own terms. Just because you need to wind down or pivot a project doesn't mean it was not a success. There can be a lot of shame and guilt associated with ending or winding down a project, but you can reframe this cultural conditioning by focusing on what you've learned, what you are grateful for, and what lessons you will carry into your next project.

Reflect on the following questions:

I'm proud of this project because . . .

The skills I learned or honed with this project were:

This project surprised me because:

Three big lessons I learned from this project that I will carry into the next one are:

1.

2.

3.

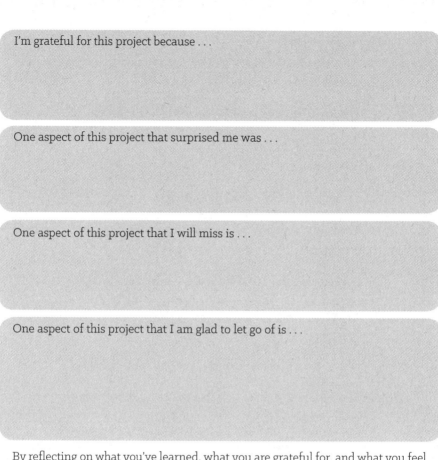

I'm grateful for this project because . . .

One aspect of this project that surprised me was . . .

One aspect of this project that I will miss is . . .

One aspect of this project that I am glad to let go of is . . .

By reflecting on what you've learned, what you are grateful for, and what you feel proud of, you'll get a sense that "success" and "failure" can feel arbitrary—what's important is that you are learning and growing as a creative person.

Transition Planning

If you decide it's time to end a project, making a plan to wrap things up will help you accept what is ending, reflect on what worked, and build a greater sense of relief and satisfaction about the project as a whole.

Refer back to the "workback timeline" template in the first section and use it to plan a wind down/project transition.

Start with your desired end date and make a timeline from there.

Your timeline might include:

- Inform your suppliers, employees, collaborators, customers, and community of your decision to end the project

- Give notice to studio space or workspace if moving out of a physical location

- Pay any outstanding bills

- Submit and collect any outstanding invoices

- Meet with a lawyer and accountant to go over any financial or legal considerations

- Set and communicate last day to accept orders/new work

- Set and communicate last day to fulfill orders or when all work will be delivered

- If you can afford it, host a closing thank you party or event

- Sell or donate any supplies or tools you will no longer need

- Send out a "thank you" note to your mailing list or community

- Update project website and social media to inform visitors about your project's end or transition

- Let your community know what is next, how they can support you, and encourage them to keep in touch

The beautiful part of being a DIY creative, and part of the DIY community, is that it is always part of you. Your experiences bringing a creative project to life, however or big or small, will shape you and continue to impact your life in ways you may not expect in the future. As you move on to the next project or phase in your life, honor the relationships that you made, the support you received, the community built, and yourself for trusting your vision and the energy you put into creating something that is uniquely yours in this world.

Chapter Eleven Checklist

○ Assess if continuing with this project is in the best interest of your creative energy, your personal life and financial health, and the original mission of the project

- If you find that you are sacrificing more than you are generating reward, you might consider ending or changing the project

○ Create and execute a transition plan to tie up loose ends, show appreciation for yourself and your supporters, and pivot towards new ideas and passions!

RESOURCES

This workbook is a gateway for you to access the world of resources that are available for your specific project. These are some of my favorites that I have found especially helpful and inspiring.

Career and Business Planning

The $100 Startup: reinvent the way you make a living, do what you love, and create a new future

Chris Guillebeau

A fun, innovative guide to launching and growing a business on your terms

The Artist's Guide: Making a Living Doing What You Love

Jackie Battenfield

Excellent career planning guide for all types of creative people

Art/Work: everything you need to know (and do) as you pursue your art career

Heather Darcy Bhandari and Jonathan Melber

Practical considerations for launching your career as an artist

Craft, Inc.

Meg Mateo Ilasco

Turning your creative hobby into a business

Creative, Inc.

Joy Deangdeelert Cho and Meg Mateo Ilasco

Planning and organizing your freelance career

From Chaos to Creativity

Jessie Kwak

Time and task management for creative people with creative projects.

The Handmade Marketplace

Kari Chapin

How to launch a craft business

How to Not Always Be Working: A toolkit for creativity and radical self-care

Marlee Grace

Dancer, entrepreneur, and podcaster reflects on how to build healthy boundaries between your work, life, and job.

Music Success in Nine Weeks

Ariel Hyatt

Guide to setting goals and achieving them for bands and musicians

Pineywood Atlas

pineywoodatlas.com/

A catalogue of unconventional, emerging, and accessible artist residencies across the United States that offer resources for creatives who want to learn more about artist residencies and communities.

Punk Rock Entrepreneur: Running a Business Without Losing Your Values

Caroline Moore

A guide to launching your own business using DIY methods that allow you to begin from wherever you are, right now.

YearCompass

A free resource to help you check in with your values and goals annually.

https://yearcompass.com/

Your Art Will Save Your Life

Beth Pickens

Considerations for building a sustainable creative practice while dealing with institutions like funding and graduate school.

Money and Finance

The Creative Professional's Guide to Money

Ilise Benun

Accessible advice for managing your money

The Crafter's Guide to Pricing Your Work

Dan Ramsey

The Graphic Artists Guild Handbook: Pricing & Ethical Guidelines

Invaluable information about contracts, pricing and legal rights for graphic artists.

Unfuck Your Worth: Overcome Your Money Emotions, Value Your Own Labor, and Manage Financial Freakouts in a Capitalist Hellscape

Faith G. Harper, PhD

A guide to overcoming emotional barriers around money

Legal Considerations

American Society of Composers, Authors and Publishers (ASCAP)

http://www.ascap.com/

US-based performance rights organization for musicians and composers

The Legal Guide for the Visual Artist

Tad Crawford

A reference book covering basic legal issues for anyone working in the visual arts.

LegalZoom

legalzoom.com/

Services and templates for contracts, business incorporation, protecting your intellectual property, and more.

Volunteer Lawyers for the Arts

http://www.vlany.org/

Based in NYC, VLA offers legal classes, workshops, and advocacy for artists and arts nonprofits.

Organizations

Craftcation Conference/Dear Handmade Life

https://dearhandmadelife.com/craftcation-conference/

Annual conference bringing together creative entrepreneurs from around the country, as well as a blog offering business advice and inspiration.

Creative Commons

creativecommons.org

Nonprofit organization that enables the sharing and use of creativity and knowledge through free legal tools

Etsy

http://www.etsy.com

Online marketplace for handmade items that offers extensive education resources for its sellers.

The Foundation Center

http://www.foundationcenter.org/ and http://grantspace.org

Extensive database for researching grants from public and private institutions and offers classes, workshops and resources for learning about fundraising, including sample proposals.

Fractured Atlas

http://www.fracturedatlas.org

Professional development, insurance, fiscal sponsorship and resources for artists in all disciplines.

Freelancers Union

http://www.freelancersunion.org/

Insurance, advocacy, resources and support for independent workers.

The Graphic Artists Guild

https://www.graphicartistsguild.org

National networking, advocacy and professional development organization for graphic artists including designers, illustrators, cartoonists and digital artists

The Independent Publishing Resource Center

http://www.iprc.org

Workspace, classes and community for all types of self-publishers located in Portland, Oregon

The New York Foundation for the Arts

http://www.nyfa.org

Resources, professional development, fiscal sponsorship and information for artists in all disciplines, no matter where they live. For researching grants, services and opportunities check out NFYA Source at http://www.nyfa.org/source

SCORE

score.org

Nonprofit offering small business counseling and mentoring.

Small Business Association

http://www.sba.gov

Support, resources, mentoring and links to government forms and agencies for those launching or running a small business.

US Copyright Office

copyright.gov

Register a copyright and find more information about projecting your intellectual property.

Strengths tests

high5test.com

Gallup: gallup.com/cliftonstrengths

ABOUT THE AUTHOR

Eleanor C. Whitney is a feminist writer, musician, and editor living in Brooklyn. She has built community and content strategy for startups and arts organizations including Axiom, Managed by Q, Dev Bootcamp, Shapeways, and the Brooklyn Museum. She holds an undergraduate degree from Eugene Lang College, an MPA from Baruch College, and is currently pursuing an MFA in creative nonfiction at Queens College. Her first book, *Quit Your Day Job*, is a practical field guide for managing a creative business. She's currently working on her next book, Riot Woman, a collection of feminist essays, and is the host of a podcast of the same name. She loves to punch out her writer's block at her local boxing gym.